CLOSING
THE BACK DOOR
OF THE CHURCH

CLOSING
THE BACK DOOR
OF THE CHURCH

PREVENTING LOSS FROM THE LOCAL CHURCH
AND THE WHOLE CHURCH

RON KALLMIER AND ANDY PECK

CWR

CONTENTS

We can't fully explain why, but there has been a rapid change in patterns of church attendance and allegiance. Evangelism is vital for the health of churches large and small – but why are so many existing people leaving?

As it grapples with the effects of the growth of individualism and how it impacts churches just like yours this book will take you beyond the superficial, help you to understand what has been happening and what responses are appropriate, and in so doing show you how to avoid the revolving door syndrome in your church.

Declan Flanagan, Chief Executive of Rural Ministries

This is a significant contribution to the debate on what a healthy church looks like. It is well written, thoughtful and provides practical advice on how the 'back door' of churches can be closed. I would strongly commend it to all those who lead local churches.

Bishop Mike Hill, Bishop of Bristol

Just talking about a sinking church will not stop it from drowning.
God is always looking to help people who do not give up and are willing to dive in and start rescuing it.
This book will give you some diving instructions !

Ishmael, Travelling family ministry, author, songwriter, missioner and Deacon at Chichester Cathedral

Lionel Fletcher, a well-known Anglican evangelist in the 1930s, said 'All churches grow, we must just stop them leaking'. *Closing the Back Door of the Church* puts this thought to us in a dynamic and relevant way, highlighting not only the problems but offering practical ideas and solutions on how one might face this issue and begin to deal with it.

I've found this stimulating and thought-provoking as it is an issue the Church today must deal with.

Laurence Singlehurst, Cell UK and author of *Sowing, Reaping, Keeping: People-sensitive Evangelism*

FOREWORD

I recall a conversation with a friend concerning the significant numbers of people who (for one reason or another) give up attending church. I pointed out that the picture was not all gloom and doom, citing the steady growth of a large number of churches and the effectiveness of programmes such as the renowned Alpha course. My friend acknowledged the point, but then made a telling comment: 'Yes, there is some growth in places. But it's a bit like sitting in the bath with the taps on and the plug out.'

This book is about understanding why the plug is out and – most importantly – how we might attempt to put it back in again.

It won't surprise you to know that the book looks at how we 'do' church and, connected to this, how we can 'be' church more effectively. It is not written by theorists but by two people who have experienced church leadership first hand. Based on his research and experience, Ron Kallmier, the Director of Training (2006–2009) at CWR, launched a workshop entitled Closing the Back Door of the Church. The response was greater than anticipated, and Ron realised that here was an issue which perplexed many leaders. His co-author, Andy Peck, is himself an experienced pastor who understands the 'plug out/open back door' problem that exists in local churches. Ron and Andy's thoughtful collaboration draws on some keen insights from a wide variety of sources to help us gain a greater understanding of why people leave church and how the attrition can be addressed with both sensitivity and urgency.

Graham Tomlin puts his finger on a large part of the problem in his insightful book, *The Provocative Church*:

> *To put it bluntly, church attendance sometimes doesn't seem to make any great difference to people's lives. If going to church and calling myself a Christian makes almost no discernable difference to the way I live my life, spend my money or use my time, then it is not surprising if my friends who are not Christians are not that interested in finding out any more about it.*[1]

Putting it simply, we need to be more credible disciples if we are to create provocative communities that will be difficult to ignore, attractive to join and harder to leave.

I find *Closing the Back Door of the Church* helpful for a number of reasons. Firstly, it asks the right questions. Why do people leave the Church? Or, to bring it nearer home, why do they leave *our* church? Are there things that we do (or don't do) that could cause people to lapse? Are there early warning signs that we can identify? Can we change our structures in such a way that makes it easier for people to share their restlessness before they consider leaving?

Secondly, the book comes up with some credible answers. Taking account of changes in culture and recognising that when it comes to church it's not a case of 'one size fits all', the authors offer some workable ideas that will help to shape strategies for local churches.

Thirdly, this is a practical book. Each chapter concludes with some sharply focused questions, helping leaders to think constructively about taking a fresh look at how effective communities of faith are built, communities that take into account people's differences and their various levels of understanding and need.

The authors avoid the current trend of claiming to discover some lost element of the gospel, hidden to the Church for centuries but (miraculously) revealed to a chosen few in the last ten years. Instead, they offer some thoughtful approaches to a clear and present danger. It comes down to a single important question: how can we become more effective at growing disciples that stay the course?

I like the mood of this book, as it avoids both the counsel of despair and the language of triumphalism.

Bishop Tom Wright retells the story of the late Lesslie Newbigin, who was asked how he viewed the future; was he optimistic or pessimistic? 'I am,' he said, 'neither an optimist nor a pessimist. Jesus Christ is risen from the dead!'[2]

A living hope, based on the living Christ remains the source of our strength.

Ian Coffey, Director of Leadership Training, Moorlands College
Summer 2009

INTRODUCTION

Andy Peck

In 2006 Ron Kallmier, Director of Training at CWR, advertised a workshop called Closing the Back Door of the Church, which considered why people were leaving local churches, and the Church in general. Day courses are a regular part of CWR's ministry, alongside the longer and more concentrated counselling courses. All are held at Waverley Abbey House near Farnham, Surrey, the home of CWR since 1987. Ron expected about twenty people, so he was surprised and delighted when more than eighty came.

Since then the workshop has run seven times, with a limit of forty people to facilitate interaction. The course has been adapted as reflections from participants have shaped Ron's thinking, and as he has discovered new ways of presenting the material. The course has drawn church leaders, church members, and some who have stopped attending church altogether. Most have come from the UK, and a few from overseas. For many, losing people from their church was a live issue. Many were hungry for answers, fearful that the local church they know and love would not survive unless something was done.

This book is based on those workshops. The first section looks at why people leave local churches, and what can be done about this. We then ask why people leave 'the Church' in general – ie leave one church but never join another. We end by looking at how some churches in the UK are making a positive response to this reality, and preparing for an exciting future.

Ron invited me to help with this book when the demands of directing CWR's training department reduced the time available to write. It says a lot about his generous spirit that he has left me to take care of his 'baby' with little interference, and given me free rein to add my own material too.

The reason for the workshops – Ron Kallmier

A SEASON OF GLOBAL CHANGE

During the past twenty years, the worldwide Church has been undergoing arguably its most major transformation in 2,000 years. For many decades the Church had been growing in Africa, Asia and South America while it has been declining in Europe, and this trend has accelerated dramatically over the past twenty years: during this time significant sections of the Church in the West, including many local congregations, have suffered a contraction of membership and attendance. This is particularly true of traditional Protestant denominations. In many of the declining churches the average age is increasing, causing added concern for the medium-to-long-term viability of these congregations.

Over that same twenty-year period I have been reading, reflecting and talking to church leaders in the UK and in Australia endeavouring to gain the broadest possible picture of the Church in the West. From what I have learned, some church leaders are unclear about the philosophical and cultural changes that have taken place in our Western culture, and those who are aware of such changes are troubled by them. For many of us in Christian leadership, the current situation poses the question: 'What can be done about it?'

Undoubtedly, the Church has 'leaked' members at a disconcerting rate in many Western churches over the last three decades. The slow but steady decline of church attendance which began in the 1960s has gathered pace. Simultaneously, the Church's influence in society has been marginalised or repudiated as the lingering influence of old Christendom has dissipated.

One of the defining moments which stimulated my concern for the future of the Church occurred thirty years ago. I was in full-time Christian education and youth ministry as a denominational leader of the Churches of Christ based in Sydney, Australia. One of my most satisfying duties was to lead inter-church Christian youth camps. Even in those days, numerical decline was beginning to affect the Church. I was deeply concerned that young people were finding it difficult to connect with activities in the local churches. Many were Christians, or from Christian families. The analogy that came to mind was of a fast-running stream with the young people on one side and the Church on the other – and no stepping-stones between. I remember asking my colleagues, 'How can we make the Church accessible to these young people?'

For many of us in local church leadership during the last twenty years, the task of charting our church's future is complicated by an avalanche of new circumstances, and by the accelerating pace of change both inside and outside our churches. For many of us, simply understanding what is going on is difficult. To stay true to our calling as Christian leaders trying to follow the teachings of Jesus, amidst the tangle of changes happening around us, is quite daunting.

One of the major contributors to church decline is the effect of our changing world. Its influence is profound and pervasive, and not all church members are aware of it. But those who do not understand how global changes will affect their local churches will have to face up to them. If we cannot see that our changing world and culture are intruding into the lives of church people, we will have a 'blind spot' that prevents us from addressing the 'back-door' problem – for the local church, and the worldwide Church.

There are challenges confronting the Western Church here and now. Others are looming in the near future. At the same time, however, there are blossoming opportunities for the Church in this new era. The prevailing changes will shape the everyday world of people who are in the Church, or were in the Church – or who we would like to see in the Church. We fail to recognise the speed of change at our own risk, in the short term and the long term.

As church leaders, we mustn't have a hazy view of the state of our world: we must be clear about the culture in which our church people, and their neighbours, live and struggle. Christian leaders must be better informed about local and global trends. Then we can discern the opportunities and problems that will confront our local churches in the next five to ten years. We cannot foresee it all, but we must learn and pray and plan. Otherwise, we will still be preparing for what has passed away! In that event, what happens in our churches will be seen as increasingly irrelevant to ordinary, weekday life. Clearly the task is not a simple one, especially when we are trying to follow the guidance of Scripture.

This is a time for churches to empower their people with the same spirit and wisdom as the men of Isaachar, who 'understood the times and knew what Israel should do' (1 Chron. 12:32). We must do in-depth research, and pray for guidance. We must use our eyes and ears to understand what people inside and outside the Church are communicating to us, verbally or in other ways. More than ever we need to seek the wisdom and power of the Holy Spirit who birthed, directs and sustains this unique body called the Christian Church.

About this book – Andy Peck

When Ron asked me to help with this book, I was delighted. The Church, and its growth and decline, have been concerns throughout my working life. In 1991 I travelled to the USA to see what could be learned from visiting some of the 'mega-churches' there, and I had the privilege of meeting staff of Chicago's Willow Creek Community Church, a church that UK church leaders were beginning to learn from. A decade later I returned to visit another 'mega-church', Saddleback Community Church in Orange County, California, and I've tried ever since to keep abreast of such influences on the UK Church.

In the UK I've been able to preach in over fifty churches and work as a pastor in three of them: in Bournemouth, Southampton and Banstead, Surrey. I have enjoyed Christian Brethren worship, which I grew up with on the Isle of Wight, in two Baptist churches, conservative and charismatic in an independent 'seeker-targeted' church (aiming to reach those who are outside the Church, but seeking God) and in a New Wine Anglican church. My regular podcast listening includes services from a mega-church in Grand Rapids, Michigan, and a former Pentecostal church in Redding, California. All of which means I am either eclectic in my worship, or thoroughly mixed-up! What unites all these churches is the centrality of a Bible-based understanding of life, and a desire to make Christ known to those inside and outside the Church.

Prior to becoming a CWR tutor I was deputy editor of the London-based *Christianity* magazine, and I currently host *The Leadership File*, a weekly programme on London's Premier Christian Radio. Both jobs have given me a unique insight into the Church in the UK and overseas, opportunities to meet Christian leaders, and an inside track on how the Church is responding to the challenges of the late twentieth and early twenty-first century.

Perhaps you are reading this because your interest was sparked by the title: maybe because people have left your church and you are wondering why; or because you know why and don't know what to do about it. Maybe you are aware of the anti-Church trends in the UK and many other

Western nations. Maybe you see the signs, and anticipate problems in your own church?

CHURCH DECLINE

The secularisation of Britain has been well documented. Although some sections of the media seem gleeful about decreasing church attendance, and perhaps exaggerate the extent to which Britain is a 'godless nation', there is plenty of hard statistical evidence of this decline. The organisation Christian Research found that one million people left the Church in the UK between 1989 and 1998, with a further half-million from 1998 to 2005.[1] Peter Brierley's book based on these figures, *Pulling Out of the Nosedive*, suggests we can be grateful that people are not leaving the Church as quickly as they were.

Monica Furlong writes: 'In the twenty years between 1980 and 2000 the Church of England suffered a 27 per cent decline in church membership. The Roman Catholic Church suffered a similar decline in the same period in Mass attendance.'[2] The major denominations face the biggest declines, with just Baptist churches holding their own during this period. Even the 'New Churches', which were growing, have levelled off in numbers. The sector seeing growth during this period was the Black-majority churches in London, and the Orthodox Church (partly because of a rise in immigrant numbers).[3]

Some want to put a more positive spin on these figures. Certainly we must factor in church attendance patterns: in many Anglican churches, attending church once a month would not be uncommon, and the statistics probably miss this. The figures may exaggerate the loss because Anglican churches, which represent the largest denomination, might choose to underestimate their attendance in order to reduce their quota within the diocese. In *The Empty Church Revisited* (2003) Robin Gill, reflecting on the lower attendances in the Church of England, writes: 'The decline in membership may partly reflect a membership role that is more tightly kept (to avoid excessive local quotas).' He concludes, however: 'At every point the Church of England appears to be in chronic decline.'[4]

Do these attendance figures reflect a true picture of the Church in the UK? In a previous generation many would attend church because it was 'the done thing', along with paying taxes, giving to charity, and listening to the

Queen's Speech on Christmas Day. Many people went to church with little or no genuine faith in God or intention to follow Jesus, but happy enough to be 'OK for heaven' (as they saw it). Today, people are far less likely to be in church conforming to social convention, or for 'show'. Maybe today's low church attendance is merely an obvious demonstration of what has existed for a long time.

RELIGIOUS DECLINE

This decline in church attendance is part of an overall decline in religious affiliation in the UK, as the figures below indicate.

Population in the UK attending church:
1979 – 12%, 1989 – 10%, 1998 – 7.5% (Christian Research)

Percentage who:	1964	1970	1983	1992	2005
'belong' to a religion	74	71	55	37	31
do not 'belong' to a religion	3	5	26	31	38

Source: *British Social Attitudes* (2006/7)[5]

Professional research in 2006 by Tearfund found that two-thirds (66% – 32.2 million people) of the UK have no connection with any religion or church.[6] In independent research, the Church Army suggest 40% have no connection with a church.[7] In August 2003, 18% of the British public said they were a practising member of an organised religion, and 25% that they were members of a world religion. According to these results, one fifth of self-declared members of a religion would also not describe themselves as practising that religion.[8]

Martyn Percy believes that a decline in religion does not mean a declining interest in spirituality:

> *There seems to be little evidence that religion is becoming less of a feature within contemporary culture. For example the interest in spirituality – religious and sacred sentiment outside the immediate control of formal religion – has been burgeoning for many years in the Western world. It would seem that, in the midst of consumerism*

*and secularization, people are turning more than ever to texts and
techniques that inspire and enchant. This appears to result in the
continual (if somewhat diffuse) infusion of inchoate spirituality
at every level of society, suggesting that society, no matter how
atomized and incoherent, persists in the quest for sacral meaning
amidst the everyday reality of mundane modernity.*[9]

But even with these necessary caveats, the figures are discouraging.
Fewer people are attending church, and many in Britain are not looking to
the Church to meet their spiritual needs.

This book aims to help Christians who want to grapple with the issues
surrounding church decline, assess their own situation, and decide what
to do if their church is not to follow the sad statistics. If you have been on
one of CWR's church attendance workshops, the flavour of the book will be
familiar, but much of the material will not. We hope it will be used by staff
teams, leadership teams, diaconates and PCCs – perhaps as a discussion
starter. In many churches hard decisions will need to be taken if they are to
halt the decline, meet the needs of the present, and also – most importantly
– adapt to the demands of the future.

CWR exists to support the Church, and we do not believe it is our
role to endorse any particular view of the future. In any case, this subject
does not lend itself to a 'seven steps to solve the problem' style, so we offer
several options and leave you to judge which are appropriate or desirable
models for your situation – praying that God may guide your steps as you
seek His direction.

But first, we need to make sure we are talking about the same thing.

MIND YOUR LANGUAGE

What do we mean by 'church'?

The title *Closing the Back Door of the Church* conveys the image of church leaders suddenly realising that people are slipping out of the back of the building, as they welcome new arrivals at the front. The numbers attending the CWR workshop suggest it's a title that has worked well. But like any word picture, it can be taken too far. We need to underline at the very start that while the *church building* is often associated with the *church* that meets there, they are not the same. Indeed a focus on church as 'the building' and not 'the people' can mean we fail to appreciate what 'church' really means.

In this book we use the word 'church' in its New Testament sense. The Greek word *ekklesia* – literally 'assembly, congregation, council'– is the traditional term for the Christian Church. The Latin form *ecclesia* is used in English to denote either a particular local group of Christians, or the whole body of the faithful. In the book of Acts, which describes the activity of the apostles just after Jesus ascended into heaven, the apostles used this common Greek word to denote a gathering of those who were followers of Jesus Christ. Following Jesus had a particular meaning in those days, linking with Jesus' practice of calling the twelve apostles and others to be with Him, and learn from Him how to live a new kind of life in the kingdom of God. *Ekklesia* denoted people who had embraced Jesus as the One who had ultimate say over their lives and were willing to let Him teach them how to live in this world, and trusting Him for the world to come.

This needed teasing out of course, and the New Testament epistles express what following Jesus would mean for Jews and Gentiles alike as the message of Jesus was preached across the Roman world. The Gospel writers – Matthew, Mark, Luke and John, the apostle Paul, Peter, Jude, and the writer to the Hebrews – outline the implications of following Christ for the people they led and served in the first century, so that those who gathered in Christ's name remained communities committed to believing and living an orthodox and authentic gospel. The New Testament writers explain how this new faith followed on from the Old Testament, and also in places diverged from it. They explain what it meant for Jesus' Lordship to be known in a pagan world, where the Roman emperor Caesar was regarded as 'Lord'.

In that day there were no church buildings, these gatherings typically assembling in a larger home of one of the believers. In *Houses that Change the World: The Return of the House Churches*[1] Wolfgang Simson argues that these house groups were no more than twelve to fifteen in number, but in truth we do not have records, merely estimates based on the sizes of the larger houses in those days. There would be typically just one church in a town, or perhaps a number of house churches in a city – all united spiritually despite any geographical separation, and recognising the apostles' right to teach and explain the doctrines of the faith.

This trip down a biblical memory lane is simply to underline that when we talk of 'Church' today, according to the Bible we are referring to people who name Jesus as their ruler in life, and have indicated their desire to follow Him publicly. If we accept that the Bible is God's revelation then we will understand 'Church' the way He wants us to understand it, rather than the way its meaning has developed historically. And we will refrain from being dogmatic about matters where Scripture is silent or allows liberty of interpretation.

In the context of 'closing the back door', it is worth underlining the following:

- Some people leave the church (ie the physical premises of the church), but were never part of the Church spiritually, even if they said they were.
- Leaving a local church does not necessarily mean leaving 'the Church'. Someone who has left may still name Jesus as their leader in life, and so still be part of the universal Church. It may be unwise to stop meeting with other Christians, and it may lead to a drift away from a vital faith – but it doesn't mean that people who have left a church cease to be believers, or part of God's family.
- Many of our church gatherings today are probably different from the Early Church gatherings. In those days most of those gathered, if not all, would have been believers. In many settings, identifying with a church would have provoked ridicule or persecution, so that only those who were truly committed would attend.
- Many churches today consciously welcome people of no faith, struggling faith and other faiths to their public services. If and when

some of this fringe 'leave the church' they will often have different reasons from those who regard themselves as Christians.

- 'Closing the back door' refers to initiatives that churches can follow to prevent the flow of people from a local church, but as we shall see there are some factors we can do nothing about.

- 'Church' always means a gathering of people. So while we might use 'the Church' as shorthand to refer to social trends, or 'Church doctrine' to refer to beliefs, it is dangerous to use statements such as 'Our church thinks …' or 'Our church is active in …' The Church is made up of individuals, so a spectrum of opinion is likely on many matters.

- The concept of 'the local church', which presumes many churches separate from one another, is not biblical. In this book we accept the reality of independent local churches; but we do not accept that the denominational or doctrinal divisions between churchgoers, who often have very similar beliefs, is a good thing.

This attempt at a biblical definition of 'Church' is essential, because many people in Britain have a skewed understanding of what the Church is about. Britain is still known as a 'Christian country'. The Queen is the head of the Church of England, and still involved in the appointment of bishops. Bishops in that Church sit in the House of Lords. We have thousands of buildings known as 'churches' in cities, towns and villages across the countries that make up the United Kingdom. Many in our nation would claim to be Christians, and in the 2001 census just under 72% described themselves as 'Christian'.[2]

We have to distinguish between what might be termed the 'trappings of Christendom', and real Church life as understood in the New Testament. When the term 'the Church' is used, in the media and even in Christian circles, it rarely reflects the glory of that company of people joined to Christ and awaiting His return. Our concern in this book is not so much that fewer people 'come to church', but rather that true believers in Jesus are not able to continue in fellowship with other believers; and that many people rule out the possibility of finding in the Church answers to the questions that trouble them, or solutions to the issues they face in life. The authors of this book believe that churches can and should change; should communicate an authentic gospel which draws people under God's grace into a living relationship with God; should be part of a community in which His Lordship is known, and growth in Him is encouraged; and that such growth in God's grace should benefit the formal and informal communities in which Christians find themselves.

Good news

Although the statistics of church attendance in the UK may seem gloomy, it is worth acknowledging with gratitude the many signs of Christian life. Over two million people in the UK have attended an Alpha course. Alpha is a fifteen-session introduction to the Christian faith. Based at Holy Trinity Church, Brompton, west London, the course has been exported worldwide, with estimates of thirteen million having attended an Alpha course. Some of those people will have found their way through the front door of a church, and many have come into a living relationship with God. 'Christianity Explored' and the 'Y course' have also been used successfully to help people grasp the basics of the Christian faith.

Many sectors of the Church have woken up to the need to reach out to their communities, helping those outside Church realise that Christianity really is good news. To pick out one of many such attempts, the Eden Project in Greater Manchester is an initiative of the Worldwide Message Tribe (now The Message Trust) which has led to the planting of ten small Christian communities in areas of deprivation. These have brought significant reductions in crime and vandalism, such that local house prices have improved after decades of decline. According to the *Manchester Evening News*,[3] 'Drawing donations from thousands of people and businesses – many of them non-Christian – The Message has a £2.5m annual budget, employing 75 full-time staff and marshalling 300 volunteers. Though they do not go for the hard-sell, The Message is also responsible for part of the recent rise in church attendance in Greater Manchester.'

We need to note too that the decline in church attendance is a largely Western phenomenon. According to the Center for the Study on Global Christianity at the Gordon-Conwell Theological Seminary in South Hamilton, Massachusetts, USA, every major religion except Islam is declining in Western Europe.[4] The drop is most evident in France,

Sweden and the Netherlands, where church attendance is less than 10% in some areas.

Worldwide, the trend is different. Christianity is ranked as the largest religion in the world today, with approximately two billion adherents. In parts of the world, the Church is growing rapidly: Brazil, Argentina, South Korea, parts of Africa, China – and India, where recent growth has been phenomenal.

As we shall see in the course of this book, non-church attendance may not say a great deal about someone's spiritual life. According to church statistician George Barna, in his book *Revolution*,[5] some twenty million people, dubbed 'Revolutionaries', live 'a first-century lifestyle based on faith, goodness, love, generosity, kindness, and simplicity', and 'zealously pursue an intimate relationship with God' – but never attend church.

One website, www.notinchurch.com, puts it like this:

> *We would describe ourselves as Christian. If pressed for a fuller description we could use terms such as evangelical, charismatic, bible believing, possibly fundamentalist in a traditional way.*
>
> *Over the years we have been involved in youth ministry and youth clubs, involved in concert promotion, involved in organising large scale missions such as Billy Graham Satellite Missions, preaching in local churches and involved in local area missions.*

But they are not found in church on a Sunday!

We may question the wisdom of believers avoiding church, but it is a phenomenon we cannot ignore when considering the topic of church membership.

Your church

Whatever we think the Bible says about Church, and however well informed we may be about statistics of churchgoing, my guess is that we all think of 'church' as the place where we worship, or perhaps as a composite of the churches we have attended. As we shall see, many people are turned off Christianity, or church attendance, because of their personal response to a particular local church. If we think they are foolish to judge the whole

Church on one expression of it, my suspicion is that this is pretty common for us all. In this book you will have to forgive us for needing to talk in generalities about 'the Church' when your church may be nothing like that. We know that Church can be much better and much worse than what we describe, but as authors we need to show the gap between the Church as she is now and what she will be when Christ returns. You will make your judgment on whether we have been unfair, or skewed in our description; but we hope you understand the need to spend some time examining the patient's wounds if we are to have any hope of providing an appropriate diagnosis – and suggesting a cure.

Questions for discussion

1. When you hear the word 'church', what is the first image that comes into your mind?
2. Are you aware of a decline in Christianity in Britain (or the country you know best)?
3. Do you know of churches where numbers have declined? Do you know of people who have left the Church and not returned?
4. Concerning church attendance, how big a problem is the Church in the UK facing?
5. How big a problem is declining attendance in your church?

WHY HAVE PEOPLE LEFT OUR CHURCH?

In this chapter we shall look at reasons why people leave a local church. Some of the reasons reflect our experience, others were suggested by people who attended our church attendance workshop. You may think you definitely know why people have left, and are wondering what you can do about it. But it's useful to consider the range of reasons outlined in this chapter, and to ask yourself: 'Do I really know why people have left?' Many leavers feel very awkward about saying exactly why they are going, especially when talking to full-time staff at the church. So unless those leaving have been able to talk to a third party, and possibly anonymously, you may not actually know: the real reason may be buried beneath plausible-sounding ones. And sometimes people fool themselves: they can't come to terms with the reason. To quote Gregory House in *House*, a US TV medical drama, 'Everybody lies'– if only to themselves. Leavers may well have *a* reason for leaving, but that doesn't mean it is *the* reason for leaving.

Asking 'why' is also useful because many churches are not good at self-assessment. They can be a bit like a dysfunctional family: so used to oddballs with weird habits that it is only when an outsider remarks on our strange behaviour that we can see how idiosyncratic we are. The following list of reasons may have that effect on you: you may realise that some apply to your church, even though you wouldn't have spotted them yourself.

Finally, it may be useful to consider the issues that churches face so that you can spot potential problems and head them off. There may be something in what follows that is not a current problem in your church, but might loom large one day. Acknowledging this danger might stimulate courageous choices and awkward conversations that you or your church leaders would rather avoid – knowing that if you don't, your church attendance will go from 'numbers' to 'exodus' before you know it! The reasons for leaving church are considered under five broad categories, though they overlap considerably: personal, faith, congregational, leadership, conflict.

1. Personal reasons

We start with personal reasons, because these are the simplest to understand. By 'personal', we mean 'particular to an individual or family' rather than 'it's personal, so it's none of your business'! In general, personal reasons are easily explained without embarrassment to the person leaving.

1.1 A CHANGE OF LOCATION

According to the National Census of 2001, about 11% of the population changes its address each year. In 2006 The Royal Bank of Scotland conducted a survey which suggested that the average UK homeowner moved 2.6 times throughout their property-owning life. East Anglians seem the keenest to move, with 8% having moved more than ten times, while 20% of London residents have never moved from the first home they bought. Not surprisingly, house-moving was especially prevalent among the 35–44 age group, 90% of whom had moved at least once, with 15% of those over 45 not having moved from their first home.

Certainly many people move a short distance and stay in the same church (in 2001, 40% who moved, travelled less than a mile), but if you are in a town or city where people move on, then you will know that the 'bolt for the church door' can well happen because the removal van is coming. Inevitably, such movements cause instability: when people move, their friendships are at risk. One survey suggests that if someone has five friends in a church they are unlikely to leave, but if they have few or no friends, almost anything will spur them out of the door.[1] Therefore, it is easy to assume that church attendance decline is purely about geography, when the underlying reasons are about discontent with relationships.

1.2 A CHURCH BUILDING MOVE

People are generally happy to travel to church – gone are the days when the church in the parish was the one all parishioners attended. Today, the average Christian will pass dozens of churches to attend their own. Nick Spencer at LICC presents this picture of UK Christians:

> We travel three times further today than we did in 1952, and in 2001 we reached a rate of over 1.5 million housing transactions per year. As we're more mobile it means if we don't like the church we're going to we can travel to another one within commuting distance … This is not necessarily about a consumerist approach to church – 'church shopping', as it's frequently called – it's also down to the fact that we're doing unity better.[2]

That said, there are limits, both with the travelling time and the building location. Ron found that in Australia the average commute to church is twenty minutes, which (depending on the traffic) would take the churchgoer some distance. So if your church building moves, you may lose a few people who prefer not to travel so far for worship.

When a church building moves to another part of town that some members dislike, they may leave just because they don't fancy worshipping in an area they have traditionally looked down on. If you think that's a petty reason (and it is), imagine your church relocating to the worst part of your own town or city, and ask yourself whether all the members would move. And would you?

1.3 Work dominates

Survey after survey finds that the average Brit works harder than their European counterpart. According to the European Union's Foundation for the Improvement of Living and Working Conditions, workers in full-time jobs in the UK put in an average of 41.4 hours every week in 2007 – almost two hours more than the average among the fifteen original members of the European Union. Only workers in Romania and Bulgaria work longer, with an average of 41.7 hours a week.[3] In times of recession the long-hours culture is likely to become even worse, perhaps with the tacit understanding by employers that employees ought to be grateful they have a job, when the boss insists they work longer. The long working hours, plus commuting, means many workers arrive home fourteen hours after they left, every day.

For many, therefore, attending local church – and especially being an active member, eg joining committees or groups – has less priority than catching up on sleep and spending time with family, when the weekend arrives. In some cases, the expected burden of 'being involved' is what actually drives them away from church. It is easier to deal with guilt at not meeting the church's standards of 'commitment' by simply staying away.

1.4 Painful events in the family

Sometimes people leave because church reminds them painfully of how things used to be. After bereavement they may say, 'I just can't bear going back: that's where they used to sit every Sunday, and I just can't face that empty space.' This is understandable, though of course church is not the only place that will remind them of the loss, and a hasty decision to leave may well be regretted later on. The hope is that a loving church environment provides the comfort that is needed at such times, and this is often the case.

But for some who have faced difficult family circumstances, such as divorce or separation, the weekly interactions with people they barely know become awkward. They don't know how much others know about their distress, and more importantly how sympathetic they will be. Many have left the local church simply because they could not face this weekly trauma.

1.5 FAMILY ISSUES

People leave church because their family is unhappy. I (Andy) recall having to chat with a couple whose sixteen-year-old son had got it into his head that every Christian should be healthy and wealthy. The lad had been listening to tapes from someone in the 'faith movement', and was convinced that he was on the side of truth and the church was in error. His promotion of these views was a headache for the youth leaders, and being responsible for youth work in the church, I had to have an awkward conversation with the parents. They appreciated my viewpoint, but said they had to back their son. They, their son and his younger brother left the church a month later.

Fears that the family may be unhappy is one reason why adults with young families never start to attend in the first place. At their first service, the parents see how few children there are the same age as theirs, and never come back. This makes it especially hard for churches with few children and young people to reverse the cycle of decline: which family would want to 'stick it out' in the hope that things will change if there is a church with vibrant children's activities a short journey away?

Indeed Peter Brierley, former director of Christian Research, argues that there is a correlation between growing churches and youth work. Churches that have seen the need to strengthen their provision of children's and young people's ministry have reaped the dividends.[4]

Ron speaks of the time he attended a small inner-city church in Sydney: 'I was asked to go in and talk to them about their youth programme. So I arrived for this meeting with the leaders and said "So who have you got in your youth group?" They said there was an eighteen-year-old girl and a thirteen-year-old boy. I was thinking: "That's not a youth group!" There was no way they could start a youth group with two teenagers – it was just not going to work. It had declined to the point that it was absolutely dead, and just couldn't operate any more.'

1.6 TEENAGER DRIFT

Having done a little work on my family tree I found, like so many, that my forebears had far fewer choices than I have had in my life. My Mum's side of the family were cotton workers in the north of England, and a previous generation were miners in South Wales and Gloucestershire. My Dad's side were nurses and publicans. I was the first to receive a university education. In those days the typical young person might follow their father's profession, or take up an apprenticeship in a trade where they would remain for most of their working lives. The older generation were respected and needed by the young.

Today it is a 'young man's world' (with apologies to women). In some sectors, a young person who grasps the latest technology may well outstrip the older generation. Their earning potential does not depend on making their way up the corporate ladder. All this means that a culture has developed which is detached from the older generation. So if 'church' is perceived to be an old-fashioned, out-of-touch gathering for oldies, a wavering believer may well be tempted to jettison church attendance in favour of more interesting pursuits.

Of course, it may be countered that if a young person truly comes to faith and is taught to know and love God, any cultural gap will not matter: but the rub comes when the young person realises that the world of church has so few connections with the world of their peer group that they cannot see any way of continuing in church. Many simply give up. They may remain believers in Jesus, but they become 'church-averse believers'.

1.7 INTEGRATION DIFFICULTIES

In the 'youth culture' described above, young people are increasingly self-sufficient within their own network of peers. Whereas a previous generation would typically trust and interact with parents and older people, today's generation can, if they wish, remain in a 'peer-group bubble' all day – spending time together at school, then texting and chatting online in the evening. In his book *Mend the Gap*[5] Jason Gardner emphasises how peers trust each other, rather than adults, by recounting the story of a youth worker leading a youth group. He suggested a scenario for the class of mid-teens to think through: 'You are invited out by a nineteen-year-old. Who do you go to for advice on deciding?' They all agreed that they would go to one of their mid-teens mates, and that no one would ask the advice of an adult – especially not a parent. The youth worker then asked: 'So, how many of your friends have ever been out with a nineteen-year-old?' Silence. The point was made. Why would you trust a peer who knew nothing of what they were advising on?

If peers are generally trusting each other, rather than adults, this has huge ramifications for integrating young people into a church where respect is given to those who are older. Such a church needs to face this cultural battle head-on, and not assume that teenagers will be compliant because 'that's what we do in church'. Appointing a youth worker is only part of the answer. It can help, but we need to make sure that the youth worker aims to integrate young people into a growing life in Christ as part of the church – not merely to be entertained until they are old enough to leave.

1.8 LIFESTYLE PRESSURES

Young adults may leave the Church because they prefer to behave in ways not in keeping with orthodox church teaching and practice. Indeed they may cite 'cultural differences' or 'lack of youth-friendly content' because these sound like respectable reasons, when the real truth is that they are sleeping around, or taking drugs, or clubbing all night. Every generation probably feels that they faced the greatest temptations, and certainly a life rooted in Christ can withstand anything the world throws at it; but the present generation are vulnerable to pressures their forebears never faced. Access to pornography has never been easier: you can download it to your PC or laptop without ever having to enter a newsagent; and the intensity of 'televisual' stimulation of desire for sex and material possessions, including sophisticated advertising, means that young people today are bombarded with temptation in ways previous generations never were. Churches that don't help their young people combat these onslaughts are simply asking to lose those young people.

If someone leaves church for personal reasons, there is very little that you can do about it. Your role as a friend or leader would be to help them find an appropriate church elsewhere, and to maintain contact, perhaps by phone/text/email, in the meantime. It is more painful to acknowledge that the person's reasons for leaving stem from the local church itself.

2. Faith issues

2.1 LOSS OF FAITH

Professor Leslie Francis was planning research on why people leave the Church, and by chance he met a bishop who was adamant that the chief reason was 'loss of faith'. In the subsequent research, Francis discovered that the bishop was partly correct. It was one of the factors – but not the major one. One in three of Francis's church-leavers pointed to loss of faith as their key reason for leaving. Loss of faith was a more important reason for men, for those who left early in life, and for Roman Catholics.[6]

The range of underlying reasons for loss of faith is enormous, and they underpin many of the other reasons we consider in the next chapters. By 'loss of faith' we mean that people no longer believe in God, or Jesus; or no longer accept the narrative the Church offers to describe this world and the life to come. It may be doubt about the Bible, about who Jesus is, about the uniqueness of Jesus, about church attitudes to other faiths or those of no faith. But in some churches people may lose faith and still be made welcome. We wouldn't support a philosophy of 'that's OK, whatever you believe', but it should be possible to remain part of the church as a loss of faith is explored.

2.2 REJECTION OF INITIAL COMMITMENT

Jesus' parable of the sower reminds us that the seed, the Word of God, meets various types of soil when it is sown:

> Then Jesus said to them, 'Don't you understand this parable? How then will you understand any parable? The farmer sows the word. Some people are like seed along the path, where the word is sown. As soon as they hear it, Satan comes and takes away the word that was sown in them. Others, like seed sown on rocky places, hear the word and at once receive it with joy. But since they have no root, they last only a short time. When trouble or persecution comes

because of the word, they quickly fall away. Still others, like seed sown among thorns, hear the word; but the worries of this life, the deceitfulness of wealth and the desires for other things come in and choke the word, making it unfruitful. Others, like seed sown on good soil, hear the word, accept it, and produce a crop – thirty, sixty or even a hundred times what was sown.' (Mark 4:13–20)

Three out of the four soils fail to produce fruit, and this is a reminder that many who attend the local church will be 'non-productive'. For some, rejecting the Word comes very soon, but in the case of the person who initially receives the Word with joy but allows the cares of life to strangle the Word in them (vv.18–19), this may occur many months or years later. A change of circumstance or a crisis reveals how shallow or weak their faith really was. If Jesus expected a varied reaction to His preaching, we must expect the same when we preach!

So, for some people, non-church attendance starts when they are not functioning well in their spiritual walk with God – for whatever reason. With God off the agenda, church attendance slips. They stop coming one week, two weeks, three weeks, and before long their routine has changed so that Sunday worship does not feature at all. There may be other factors: temptation, work pressures, family pressures; but the heart of it is that they have fallen out of love with God and don't want, or know how, to return to Him.

The New Testament has its examples of this: Paul writes of Demas that 'Demas, because he loved this world, has deserted me and has gone to Thessalonica' (2 Tim. 4:10); John writes of those who 'went out from us' (1 John 2:19), and Jesus addresses a whole church (in Laodicea) which was 'lukewarm – neither hot nor cold' in its lack of enthusiasm (Rev. 3:16).

2.3 DISCOVERING WHAT FOLLOWING JESUS ENTAILS

Jesus didn't have a 'back-door' problem with His followers, which is no surprise given that most of His recorded preaching was delivered in the open air! You might say He had a 'back of the crowd' issue, but He didn't see it as problematical. People were always free to come and go, to listen to Him or not; He didn't exclude people – they excluded themselves, if they wanted. One of His hearers' key reasons for bowing out from following

Jesus was realising what He was actually about. So we read in John 6 that many stop following Him when they understand that He is starting a new community based on union with Him:

> *Jesus said to them, 'I tell you the truth, unless you can eat the flesh of the Son of Man and drink his blood, you have no life in you. Whoever eats my flesh and drinks my blood has eternal life, and I will raise him up at the last day. For my flesh is real food and my blood is real drink. Whoever eats my flesh and drinks my blood remains in me, and I in him. Just as the living Father sent me and I live because of the Father, so the one who feeds on me will live because of me. This is the bread that came down from heaven. Your forefathers ate manna and died, but he who feeds on this bread will live for ever.' He said this while teaching in the synagogue in Capernaum.*
>
> *On hearing it, many of his disciples said, 'This is a hard teaching. Who can accept it?'*
>
> *Aware that his disciples were grumbling about this, Jesus said to them, 'Does this offend you? What if you see the Son of Man ascend to where he was before! The Spirit gives life; the flesh counts for nothing. The words I have spoken to you are spirit and they are life. Yet there are some of you who do not believe.' For Jesus had known from the beginning which of them did not believe and who would betray him. He went on to say, 'This is why I told you that no-one can come to me unless the Father has enabled him.'*
>
> *From this time many of his disciples turned back and no longer followed him.*
>
> *'You do not want to leave too, do you?' Jesus asked the Twelve.*
>
> *Simon Peter answered him, 'Lord, to whom shall we go? You have the words of eternal life. We believe and know that you are the Holy One of God.' (John 6:53–69)*

We face the same situation as Jesus: some would stop attending your church if you told them what God actually requires of them. Indeed, it may be that you are losing people because your message is getting clearer and the

Spirit of God is at work, convicting people in a way that they don't like!

This is the dilemma which some churches face which have a strong (and in our view correct) emphasis on helping newcomers to connect with church. They want to be welcoming and accepting in the way that Jesus was in His earthly ministry. But to be truly authentic they have to be up-front about the costs – and of course the glorious benefits – of following Jesus. No one likes to be told 'actually, there's some small print'. Critics of the 'seeker-targeted' type of service point out that seekers must be told at some point that true Christianity requires a radical lifestyle change.

An important caveat should be added at this point, however: for years, churches have claimed that they are refusing to 'pander to outsiders', as an excuse for being insular and self-centred. Their harsh preaching has driven people away; they claim to have been 'preaching the truth', which may be true to a point, but is not the same as 'preaching Christ' who is 'the Truth' – who did not come into the world to condemn, and so always gave His listeners hope even as He exposed their sinfulness and their need for redemption.

2.4 UNRESOLVED THEOLOGICAL QUESTIONS

Although church should be a great place for us to talk through issues of faith, some find it anything but, and despair either at being unable to express how they feel, or at how the church responds when they do. Some face very big issues: 'Why didn't God heal me?' 'If He really loves me, why did I miss out on the last three jobs I applied for?' Their ultimate response may be: 'If He doesn't love me enough to do what I want, then I'm not going to go to church!'

This problem comes from a faulty understanding of what the Christian faith is about, and may reflect the kind of faith some believers were taught: the 'come to Jesus and all your problems will disappear' kind of faith. The leaver may conclude, 'Well, I tried that and it didn't work.'

How sad that no one explained to them that we live awaiting the day when all will be made well – but in the meantime, even as believers in a loving and merciful God we do daily battle with the mysteries and struggles of life. Our faith *does* unite us with the living Christ who is graciously at work in our world and teaches us to live as He did; by faith, we begin to know God's kingdom through Jesus' grace and power. But our faith is not the token for a divine slot-machine in heaven that dispenses what we want when we want it. There will always be a mystery to God's working, along with the great certainties of His love and provision. It is sad when church fails to explain that tension, or is dismissive of those struggling with their faith.

2.5 MINISTRY BURNOUT

If you thought that 'burnout' only occurs in those who make a vocation of their service, think again: many lay people experience burnout as they juggle the competing demands of family, work, leisure and church. They are desperate not to short-change God, but find they can only keep going for so long.

Ron recalls counselling one woman who worked in an office. 'She was also active in a small but shrinking church. She was doing way too much, and when I repeatedly warned that she should give something up, her reply was always that there was nobody else to do it. Eventually she crashed and had a major burnout: she was off work, she had major physical reactions, her body was 'breaking out' in sympathy! It was all about stress – she was trying to do a full-time job, raise a family, and do too much church work.'

No one should have a gun to anyone's head, and that local church would have been horrified if it had known what sort of burden they were unwittingly placing on the woman's shoulders. If I am too busy, I have made wrong choices somewhere down the line. But I also know how tough it is to say no to things I enjoy doing – especially if I feel that others around me are doing as much, or more. When someone leaves a church through burnout, there is a high likelihood that they will return, to a church somewhere. Whether they can return to the same church will depend a lot on the relationships they had before they 'crashed'. One minister who experienced burnout was able to return after appropriate recovery time, and to the church's credit was able to continue with a fruitful ministry. If only this were always the case!

3. Congregational reasons

3.1 CHANGE IN THE CHURCH'S THEOLOGY

In their books *Gone but not Forgotten* and *Gone for Good? Church Leaving and Returning in the Twenty-first Century,*[7] Philip Richter and Leslie Francis asked church-leavers why they left. They discovered that one in every five church-leavers disengaged after experiencing problems with change in the church. New hymns, new service books, new translations of the Bible, and new styles of worship all provided obstacles to churchgoers who were uncomfortable with change. Even the arrival of a new minister brought with it the challenge of unfamiliarity. Such changes were particularly difficult for older church-leavers, and for Anglicans.

Anyone who lived through church life in the UK in the 1970s will be familiar with church splits due to the impact of the charismatic movement. Those impacted said they were 'touched by God' and needed to express a 'new dimension of their faith' within the life of the church, whether this involved tongue-speaking, prophecy or healing; so, depending on their numbers and power base, they either left for another church, or formed their own. Some were told in no uncertain terms that they were not wanted.

But this is not just a 1970s phenomenon. I host a leadership programme for Premier Christian Radio and one of my guests, Mike Riches, senior pastor of Destiny City Church, Tacoma, Washington State, described how a series of events in 2000 changed his church from a conservative expository preaching church to one where healing, exorcism and other supernatural manifestations were the norm. They lost 90% of their membership in two years, largely because the leavers said they didn't want those kind of experiences in church.

These are not the only kinds of change that cause people to leave. Other examples include the changing role of women, a change in the church's constitution (for example, away from democracy), or the adjustment of the service structure to reflect a theological change. Some churchgoers have switched one independent church for another which suits their preference; others have changed denomination. When the Church of England authorised the ordination of woman priests in 1992, and began ordaining them in 1994, many Anglicans joined the Roman Catholic Church. This included some 750 Anglican clergy who came into full Communion with Rome: 450 of them were ordained as Catholic priests, and 150 of those were given special dispensation to marry.

Ron says: 'There was a church in Brisbane where the Australian denomination as a whole took a decision that they felt was totally unethical, and the senior pastor came in one Sunday and told the congregation: "I just need you to know that I am resigning as of now because I cannot be in a system that is going so much against Scripture." And the whole church of 400 said: "We are following you." And they just left the building, locked it up, went out and started again. This happened in more than one church across Australia – all because of the same issue. It's not because the members have had a fall-out with a particular church: but they say they just can't stay under this denominational umbrella any longer.'

3.2 DESIRE FOR DEEPER RELATIONSHIPS

Sometimes people leave because they long for deeper relationships than they are experiencing. In some cases, they have enjoyed a tight-knit community in the past – maybe in a church that was smaller, or where they had a few close friends with whom they could share life intimately. They feel they have had a taste of heaven, and more superficial interactions seem like hell in comparison. For others, there is just a vague desire that Christian fellowship ought to be more than they are presently enjoying.

It may be that for the individuals concerned there are good reasons why intimacy with other church members is difficult. Some have spiritual, psychological or social problems that make it hard for people to get close to them. It is sad if the church is unable to help such people to grow in maturity, but the truth is that as individuals they are emotionally draining, and there is often a collective sigh of relief when they move elsewhere.

The desire for closer relationships is a good one. It is hard to measure, and appropriate boundaries need to be in place. For example, 'intimacy' or 'transparency' are not the same as 'being in the inner circle', 'knowing the gossip' – or prying into people's private affairs. If that is what church people really want, they need to know it is not appropriate. But if what is meant by 'closer relationships' is a willingness to speak and receive the truth in love, to pray through real-life situations, to move into greater maturity, to be freed by confessing sin, to help each other deal with blind spots in an atmosphere of love and acceptance – then every church would benefit from such intimate relationships.

3.3 GREENER GRASS SYNDROME

When I was growing up on the Isle of Wight there would be an annual circus, aimed at the holiday-makers visiting the island in the summer months. Even if you weren't a big circus fan, you had to admit that the 'big top' was a great attraction for 'grockles' (Isle of Wight slang for holiday-makers) and locals alike.

A similar phenomenon can be seen in local churches: it's as if the circus has come to town. All is going smoothly until a new church springs up like a big top, independent of the established churches, perhaps with a new style of worship, a new strategy, or 'offering more' to those who attend. And unlike the circus, the new church is here to stay. It can cause untold misery as stable churches find their sheep leaving for the 'greener pasture' on offer.

It may not be a new church, but a change in emphasis or approach from one of the bigger churches in town. Perhaps one church in town is growing, so people from other churches start going there to 'get in on the action'.

The 'grass is greener in another church' syndrome is encouraged by new media, which may show us excellent preaching and worship elsewhere, leading us to undervalue the weekly services we attend. Why get out of bed to be bored by your vicar, when you can listen to your favourite preacher on your ipod, or watch them on God TV!

Our point is not to criticise new churches (though they are often planted independent of local churches) or churches whose growth challenges the status quo, but simply to emphasise that many people leave their church because they think they will gain more blessings elsewhere.

3.4 BOREDOM

Many leave church because they are bored. I doubt whether many people would admit to it, and it takes a brave (or insensitive) soul to share this with the church leadership – especially if there is one person who does most of the preaching. As one wag advised a preacher: if you don't strike oil in twenty minutes, stop boring! Perhaps above all, it is the church's services that are experienced as unappealing. Services should not define the local church, but as weekly 'set-piece events' they reflect the preferences of the leaders, and those who participate. If you feel that even the Second Coming would not replace your church's 'hymn-prayer sandwich', you know that this traditional pattern will alienate those who prefer a bit of variety. Frost and Hirsch, in *The Shaping of Things to Come*,[8] which we shall look at later, describe how they visited many churches in the Western world – in the US, the UK, Australia and New Zealand – and were amazed at how very monochrome they were.

Perhaps churches fail to tackle the real-life issues its members are facing: they are taught how to 'arrange the tabernacle in the wilderness', but not the more relevant challenge of defending their faith in a hostile, anti-Christian workplace. But boredom also comes if the members of the church are inhibited from expressing their personality as people indwelt by the Spirit; or from seeking to bring God's influence into their neighbourhood, workplaces and homes. Sadly some churches are dehumanising environments, where people feel obliged to bury who they truly are, for fear that their real selves will not be welcomed.

Essentially, boredom comes because no one has demonstrated the wonderful opportunities that life with Jesus brings. It is unlikely that Jesus' first disciples were ever bored.

4. Leadership issues

Problems with a church's congregation are closely connected with problems of the church's leadership. Leadership is difficult, and many volunteer for leadership only when others refuse to 'stand up and be counted'. So what follows should not be seen as 'leader-bashing'. If you have any sort of role as a church leader, God bless you.

4.1 OVERBEARING LEADERSHIP

Some people may have left your church because they feel the leadership is 'spiritually abusive'. This may be a perception of the leadership as a whole, or just one member – often the most senior leader.

It is important to seek balance in understanding this issue, because some may perceive the leadership to be heavy-handed when in the leaders' perception they are just trying to do their job – to show leadership. If you are not used to receiving direction or advice, then the requirement, or even the suggestion, of certain patterns of behaviour may seem unacceptable; and today's culture of 'live and let live' makes some New Testament commands seem oppressive.

But taking a necessary lead, speaking the truth in love, and sharing sometimes difficult biblical advice, are not the same as the bullying practices that are sadly prevalent in some churches. In the early years of the charismatic movement in the UK there were 'New Churches' which practised 'heavy shepherding', where it was believed that leaders were anointed by God to know how someone should live – down to the detail of where they should live, or who they should marry. Thankfully, such an authoritarian style is uncommon these days, and in general the newer churches have either adopted a more flexible structure, or withered away. But church leadership patterns can still be oppressive, and some churchgoers have felt manipulated to the extent that they have to leave to stay sane.[9]

4.2 WEAK LEADERSHIP

In addition to *manipulative* or *oppressive* leadership, *weak* leadership causes some churchgoers to leave, out of exasperation. Perhaps they don't share the leaders' vision, or they feel the leaders have taken the church in a foolish direction. Perhaps the leaders have failed to tackle issues, something we shall consider later in this chapter. Sometimes the leaving is reluctant, and comes after much discussion and soul-searching. The leaver may finally offer a 'cover' reason, such as: 'We have done all we can to adapt and adjust … we're going to a church where there's more life' – or some similar pretext.

In *Pulling Out of the Nosedive*,[10] Peter Brierley cites a survey by the Salvation Army which investigated the reasons why churchgoers said their church could or could not grow. He lists fourteen spurious reasons, which were matched against actual churches that had either grown or declined. Brierley concludes: 'What then makes a church grow? Strong leadership and clear vision! These were not just the prime factors, but were proved statistically in the study to be the key reasons.'[11]

4.3 SOLE VISION LEADERSHIP

Many churches have tried to clarify their mission and vision in pithy statements which encapsulate what they stand for. In many cases this focus has enhanced the church's energy and unity. But if the vision of the church, and especially that of the senior leader, is too narrow, it will become impossible for other visionary believers to stay. If, for example, the church's vision is to reach out to international students in the neighbourhood, you won't be inspired by this vision if God has called you to work with elderly Brits.

Whatever value there is in having a unified vision, it is vital that the leadership stays open to the gifts and interests of the individuals in the church. In *The Church Unleashed*, author Frank Tillapaugh writes: 'Unleashing our churches and our potential for personal ministry means moving away from the world's fascination with titles and external credentials. The only title that really matters is the title of Christ-one. If you wear that title, you have authority as God's ambassador.'[12] Tillapaugh assumes that everyone has a 'ministry' and argues that he, as a minister in the church, is there to ensure that each individual thrives in the ministry God has given them.

My wife and I have good friends who left their local church essentially because they had a focus others did not share, and because they felt the church showed little interest in the ministry God had given them. Sometimes, an individual's vision may not be concerned with the local church at all: it may be an impulse to serve the wider community. Many have left local churches because they perceive its outlook to be too parochial and rigid.

4.4 POOR PASTORAL LEADERSHIP

People leave church because they believe the church leaders don't care about them. The old adage 'they don't care how much you know, they want to know how much you care' is still true for many churchgoers. In some cases an individual's pastoral needs may be met, but not by the vicar or senior pastor who is deemed to be 'the expert'. At CWR we run courses on pastoral care, and volunteers often comment that their care is undervalued because they don't have the title 'Pastor' or 'Reverend' in front of their name! It can be very galling to be told 'no one visits' a person in need, when you know that they have had weekly visits for months, from yourself – an untitled lay person who is better equipped for pastoral care than the pastor!

Ron recalls a conversation with someone when he was serving in a large church, who wanted a personal visit. He told her that given the size of the congregation (around 800), if he were to visit everyone in the way she had asked, he would probably take three years to get to her!

For whatever reason, there are churches whose networks of care don't work, and people leave the church claiming 'no one cared': the saddest thing about this is that they assume God doesn't care either.

5. Conflict issues

5.1 CONFLICT

There is a big overlap between issues of leadership and issues of conflict. The latter are given specific consideration because anecdotal evidence suggests that this is a major reason for people leaving a church.

Ron says: 'A school friend of mine is a Baptist minister, involved in John Mark Ministries in Australia. He has the unenviable task of resolving church disputes across seventeen denominations in that huge country. He intervenes in these situations, conducts assessments, and discusses with the leaders, to deal with church splits and associated fall-outs. In his experience, if a church doesn't confront an issue – whether moral, financial or theological – it will occur again within six years if it is not resolved. Similarly, if a person comes to your church because of conflict and they have not dealt with it, they are likely to sow the conflict back into your church. I recall a church in our area that split, and the young couple who caused the split planted another church about 100 yards away. They took half the congregation from their original church!

Sadly I can think of at least three churches in the UK where the same type of division has occurred in the last ten years – in one case, the new church meets 50 yards from the old one!

Ron continues: 'When I was doing full-time youth work, I spoke at a weekend retreat at a church in Sydney. I walked in for the first session on the Saturday morning, looked at those present, and thought, "There is a major crisis in this group." So I didn't follow my plan, and said: "I am picking up that something is not quite right. Is there a problem in this group?" They said, "We've had a major church split." So I spent the morning trying to sort out that issue before we did anything else. We had a very good reconciliation, but it was a problem that nobody had dealt with. I wouldn't say I resolved it totally, but at least as an outsider I was able to offer some help.'

The religious editor of *The Times*, Ruth Gledhill, writes (25 August 2005):

Most churchgoers who abandon their weekly worship do so because they have had a dispute with a fellow member of the congregation. A disagreement on a range of issues, from the way the organ is played to the content of the sermon, was the reason that nearly three-quarters of respondents to a survey gave for why they felt people had left the Church. The study, which surveyed more than 500 people about why they felt worshippers left, was conducted by Spring Harvest and Care for the Family, two Christian organisations, as research for a conference next February to help leaders to retain their congregations. About 74 per cent of respondents thought that people had left the church because of disagreements with other church members, while 40 per cent said that the church did not need to be more welcoming to non-Christians. Nearly all the respondents to the research were regular churchgoers, and more than half of them had attended the same church for ten years or longer.

The conflict may be a direct 'personality clash', perhaps occasioned by a difference of opinion on a matter related to church life and doctrine. When the apostle Paul wrote to the church in Philippi he urged two women, Euodia and Syntyche, to 'agree with each other in the Lord' (Phil. 4:2). These women, who evidently worked with him in ministry, had fallen out with each other. But there are perhaps more cases in church life where there is no direct conflict, but someone has been wounded in more subtle ways. For example, a person who wishes to be the leader of the music team is bypassed because somebody else is more proficient; or a couple are keen to lead a home group, but not regarded as suitable. In the church's grand scheme such disappointments may not seem important, but they can create deep wounds which – if not dealt with early and effectively – affect other areas of church life, causing anger, resentment and bitterness at a personal level.

The book of Hebrews speaks of the 'bitter root' which may 'cause trouble and defile many' (Heb. 12:15); if a wounded person harbours bitterness and passes on their resentment to others, those others may side with them in their grievance and continue the cycle. It is always regrettable when someone leaves the church wounded, but if the person refuses to let go of their bitterness it may be better for the church in the long run; and one hopes that if they join another church, similar problems will not recur.

Resolution of conflict may be required at a number of levels. There may be a major issue such as adultery, financial impropriety or criminal behaviour; but it is just as likely to be about one individual who, for example, doesn't feel their opinion is heard. The tragedy is that feuds can be allowed to fester within a congregation for generations without being dealt with – to the point where those in dispute have forgotten the original issue!

5.2 POWER-PLAYS

A battle for power makes for compelling TV or film drama. It is less fun in the church; indeed, such 'power-plays' can throw the mildest church community into disarray. Wise leaders will know the people in the church who tend to 'throw their weight around', and will take appropriate pre-emptive action to manage situations where they suspect this 'power-player' might seek to exert undue influence.

Ron says: 'I like the story a friend told me about a traditional church with a pipe organ. They loved hymns, and some loved the old organ. An older man in the congregation was opposed to the proposal to introduce an electronic organ, and at the annual church meeting he made his point forcefully. But the church voted against his view, and decided on a new organ. Given the vehemence of his disapproval, some were concerned about how he might react. They needn't have worried: he was the first to give a donation towards the new instrument, saying: "This is my church, and I am part of it. If that's what you want, I'm going to be the first to contribute."'

Sadly, such behaviour is the exception rather than the rule. Too often those who don't get their own way leave, and take with them all that they could give the church – not just their money. And the tense atmosphere created as a result can cause others to leave, too.

5.3 PRICKLY PEOPLE

In considering those who are looking for closer relationships, we mentioned that some people have spiritual or psychological problems which make any form of closeness difficult. Such people may be described as 'prickly people', who move to a new church because they haven't resolved their issues in their last church. They arrive at your church looking forward to a fresh new start: but that can't happen because they have brought *themselves* with them. So they remain unhappy, either because they fall out with someone new, or because they find that your church won't bend to their will any more than the previous church would.

The little-read letter of 3 John describes an extreme form of this behaviour, and the writer warns the church about a particular trouble-maker:

> *I wrote to the church, but Diotrephes, who loves to be first, will have nothing to do with us. So if I come, I will call attention to what he is doing, gossiping maliciously about us. Not satisfied with that, he refuses to welcome the brothers. He also stops those who want to do so and puts them out of the church.*
> *Dear friend, do not imitate what is evil but what is good. Anyone who does what is good is from God. Anyone who does what is evil has not seen God. (3 John 9–11)*

Prickly people can be some of the hardest people to pastor, largely because their self-awareness is so poorly developed that they cannot see how their own responses to church life are creating the problem. As John Ortberg helpfully entitles his book, *Everyone is Normal Until You Get to Know Them*!

5.4 SIN

This subject is the last in the list, but don't underestimate its importance. People leave church because they want to do things they know the church wouldn't approve of.

When I was a church leader we had to ask a member of the congregation to deal with a business matter that was bringing disgrace to the church. He had advertised his building firm in the local Christian business directory, and taken money for a patio job which was clearly unfinished. A colleague and I went with him to hear the customer's complaint and to inspect the work, in an attempt to resolve the dispute. Unfortunately he refused to accept the complaint and rejected our pleas to finish the job, leaving us with no alternative but to say that he was not welcome at church Communion until the matter was resolved (this being one of the ways in which church discipline was exercised in that church). He left the church soon after – and as far as I know, the patio is still unfinished!

Of course the hope is that awareness of sin brings repentance and restoration. This is always God's intention – Christ came not to condemn us but to save us. But when someone remains defiant about their own shortcomings, it can affect the church as a whole, and we can't just 'turn a blind eye'.

In times of revival people have felt God's presence, and been convicted of sin and compelled to put things right. If your church experiences God's presence more deeply, this may cause some to leave because they cannot bear the consequent awareness of their own sin. Indeed, we should pray for this to occur increasingly in all churches.

Exercise

Look back at the headings in this chapter, and ask which ones apply to your own church, and how. Use the following notation:

   A: This definitely applies to my church now.
   B: This possibly applies to my church now.
   C: This could apply to my church in the future.

What, if anything, can you do about the issues affecting your church? Consider the advice given in this chapter, as well as other strategies. Ask God to give you wisdom in these matters.

Questions for discussion

1. Are there issues of conflict in your church that are not covered in this chapter?
2. Thinking of churches you know, especially your own, what are the main conflict issues?

HOW TO CLOSE THE BACK DOOR:

RESPONDING TO A LOSS OF PEOPLE

The last chapter may have been depressing to read. If you found that all the reasons for leaving applied to your church, maybe it's time to close the back door *and* the front door, and throw away the key! But improving any church's situation starts with identifying the problem; every church has a different situation, and it is unlikely that all the solutions suggested below will be relevant to your church.

However, it is important to anticipate potential problems, and a suggestion in this chapter may be worth considering, even if it does not directly address a need you have identified. The suggestions in this chapter can be applied in most churches by simply adjusting their focus, or modifying their practice. If these seem to be sticking-plaster solutions, when you are convinced that surgery is required, you may be right: Chapter 5 will look at more radical responses.

But before we look for solutions to the issue of losing members, there are some principles to bear in mind.

ESTABLISH THE FACTS

The first thing for any church leader to do when looking at loss of members is to establish the facts. It is easy to get a false impression of a situation, when the reality is different. In the table on the next two pages are some key questions for you to ask about your church:

1. Name of church or fellowship	
2. Location	
3. Years in existence (approximately) _____	
4. Approximate membership* in 1995	Adults _____ Under 18s _____
5. Approximate membership* in 2000	Adults _____ Under 18s _____
6. Approximate membership* currently	Adults _____ Under 18s _____
7. Which of these words describe your church's attendance over the past 10 years?	☐ Growing ☐ Stable ☐ Declining ☐ Ageing ☐ Growing Younger ☐ Consistent representation of age-groups ☐ Homogeneous ☐ Multicultural
8. Does your church currently have an organised pastoral care programme?	☐ Yes ☐ No ☐ Planned
9. Does your pastoral care programme include a systematic way of *welcoming* newcomers?	☐ Yes ☐ No ☐ Planned
10. Does your pastoral care programme include a systematic way of *integrating* newcomers?	☐ Yes ☐ No ☐ Planned
11. Do you have an active pastoral care team?	☐ Yes ☐ No ☐ Planned
12. Is the pastoral team led by the senior minister or pastor?	☐ Yes ☐ No

13. Is the pastoral team led by a paid church leader other than the senior minister?	☐ Yes ☐ No ☐ Planned
14. Is there a separate welcoming team?	☐ Yes ☐ No ☐ Planned
15. Is there a strategy in place for visiting newcomers within the first few weeks of their first attending?	☐ Yes ☐ No ☐ Planned
16. In your opinion, has the church lost people within the past five years because of dissatisfaction, disenchantment or dispute?	☐ Yes ☐ No ☐ Not sure
17. How effectively has the church responded to those who have become disaffected?	☐ Effectively ☐ Mixed effectiveness ☐ Ineffectively ☐ Issues ignored ☐ Not applicable
18. What impact has the departure of disaffected people had on the wellbeing and ministry of the church?	☐ No negative impact ☐ Some negative impact ☐ Significant negative impact ☐ Some positive impact ☐ Not applicable
19. What impact has the departure of positive, supportive people had on the life and ministry of the church?	☐ No negative impact ☐ Some negative impact ☐ Significant negative impact ☐ Not applicable
20. Does the church have specific plans for stimulating numerical growth?	☐ Yes ☐ No ☐ Not sure

*In this context 'membership' is used to signify the total number of individuals who regularly attend the major gatherings, in particular services, of the church or fellowship.

Don't panic if you don't need to

It is important to discern the difference between 'satisfactory' and 'unsatisfactory' reasons for people leaving your church. In some London churches, for example, turnover can be as high as 50% every two years. This is not necessarily a cause for sorrow, but may simply reflect the 'life stages' of those who attend. Churches in university towns will have a similar experience. Some churches carry out their ministry during the small span of time that people are with them, considering their role to be equipping people as future 'missionaries' to other churches, and to places where God will take them in the UK and overseas.

So you may conclude that there is nothing that you could reasonably have done to prevent an individual or a group of people from leaving the church. If this is your honest view, it is important not to reproach yourself, and to simply continue your ministry. That can be hard to do, especially if you were close to those who left or, conversely, they disliked/disagreed with something you said or did as a leader. It would be foolish to ignore people leaving the church, as if it meant nothing; nonetheless, if you adjusted your church to fit what all members wanted, you would be changing course every month.

Furthermore, losing people may be a necessary part of church growth. I spent three years serving as an assistant minister at a church which had some 550 members. What is often forgotten is that the man who built the church to its high levels of membership came to the church when the membership was about 50, and he lost members who were upset by his decision to remove the choir. While making no general comment on the value of church choirs, whatever is deemed to inhibit the progress of God's work – even a choir – should be removed, and there may be a loss of members before growth resumes. The gardening analogy of clearing out dead wood applies here. A church may have to accept short-term loss for the sake of long-term gain; this requires some 'spiritual bottle', and no doubt some leaders refuse change, knowing that the loss of members (some of whom might be major financial donors) could be a setback.

If you have established the facts about your church leavers, and you have the right attitude about those whose leaving you could not prevent, then you are ready to consider what you can do to improve things. Our suggestions come under the following headings of *leadership, values, communication,* and *congregational priorities.*

1. Leadership

1.1 KNOW YOURSELF AND YOUR LIMITS AS A LEADER

In the business world, it is said that workers don't 'leave a job', they 'leave a boss': dissatisfaction with the job itself is not usually the reason – more often it's the relationship with a 'difficult' manager. There is also evidence from the world of Christian missions that missionaries leave their posts because of problems with their team leader.[1]

If this is the case in these two sectors, the chances are that some who leave a church do so because of its leader. If you are a church leader, the bad news is that this may have happened already in your church – and the good news is that God still loves you, and you need to look after yourself with a view to being a better leader.

For some leaders, who believe they have laid down their lives and their right to a normal life, 'looking after yourself' sounds like 'selling out'. But self-awareness is important, so that we can know and fulfil the mission that God has given us to the best of our ability. If you learnt that a fellow Christian leader often over-indulged in food and wine, you would be rightly concerned; but ask yourself: are you diligent about the rest and refreshment *you* need? Do you try to keep yourself mentally, physically and spiritually fit for the work God has given you?

CWR, my employers and the publishers of the book you are holding, are greatly influenced by Dr Larry Crabb, author, counselling guru, and close friend of CWR's late founder, Selwyn Hughes. Crabb's thinking was foundational for Selwyn Hughes' development of the 'Waverley counselling model'. I heard Larry in person at the London School of Theology, which works with CWR in delivering its counselling courses. In a question and answer session, he was asked what was the most important skill that any counsellor requires. After a short pause, he replied that if he had to pick one he would identify 'self-awareness'. He explained that unless a counsellor is self-aware they will not know how much of their response to the counsellee is actually coming from what was said, and how much is coming from themselves. The self-aware person is able to discern this.

Any form of leadership in ministry requires us to be self-aware as we assess how we are bringing our perspectives, insecurities and weaknesses into the equation. The co-dependency between pastor and congregation is well-documented: some pastors have such a strong need to be liked, or loved, that they will do almost anything to gain the congregation's favour. If the pastor only initiates change that he or she knows the people will like, stagnation is the most likely result. Typically churches do not welcome change, so the pastor will be tempted to keep the peace and leave things as they are.

So how do you become self-aware? It is partly a matter of discovering your spiritual gifts. There are many 'self-help' guides to assist you.[2] But you can start with two rules of thumb: how are you moved to help people, and what qualities have others commended in you? How you are moved to help will give some indication of the Spirit's work within you, stirring up your gift; the commendation of others will help you know how you are building them up. Actually, you may be in a role which requires gifts that you do not have. Many vicars are supposed to lead, pastor and teach: it is very rare that one person has all three gifts, or if they do, to have all three in equal measure. So a wise leader will ask others for their advice: find someone you trust to tell you the truth.

If you are unclear about your natural strengths (and *strengths* overlap with *gifts*), the book *Now, Discover Your Strengths*[3] may help. As well as guiding you in self-assessment, the book provides a questionnaire which charts your 'signature strengths' and lists thirty-one 'character types', including achiever, competitor, communicator, learner, empathiser and maximiser. Many churches and charities have used these assessment strategies to great effect.

However, such tools are no substitute for chatting with those close to you: they can tell you how you are perceived, especially regarding your strengths and weaknesses as a leader. Your ministry is not just about *what you do*, but *who you are*, and for that you need people who care enough about you to tell you the truth – straight.

1.2 DON'T BE A 'ONE-PERSON BAND'

There have been some great but dictatorial leaders in local churches, whose insight into what God was seeking to do through their people has made their ministry well known throughout the world. Many leaders would admit, in their less guarded moments, that they live by the adage 'if you want something done, do it yourself'. But the 'one-man band' model (it is usually a man) does not sustain a ministry for the long haul; nor does it develop individuals within the church who can emulate or complement the leader – and eventually take over from them.

The New Testament has a very broad view of leadership. It specifies that:

- All Christians have a ministry
- In every church God calls some believers to be leaders
- Leaders are called to be servants
- Church leadership is always plural
- One of the leaders may be the primary leader. (For example, Acts 12:17 and 15:13–29 suggest that James is the primary leader of the Church in Jerusalem
- Leadership and ministry are to be 'gift-based': gift precedes function

A wise full-time leader will work as part of a team. In 72% of churches in the UK there is one full-time (ordained or 'recognised') leader, with 18% having more than one ordained person. The majority of these churches have a paid second person. So full-time 'team leadership', if two people are a team, is relatively rare. For most churches, 'team' means lay people with whom ideas can be shared and plans made. If the full-time person has leadership gifts then they are usually the person who drives the church forward; but in some cases the 'driver' will be a lay person, who is able to lead strategically and leave the vicar or minister to teach and pastor.[4]

If leadership is in the hands of just one person, the potential of the church is bound to be limited, and there is a danger of this one leader upsetting members.

1.3 STAY ACCOUNTABLE

'Accountability' has become something of a buzz-word within the Church. It cannot be an infallible way to keep us all on track: after all, it will only work to the extent that leaders are prepared to be transparent. But having those around us to whom we give permission to 'speak into our lives' can be a valuable antidote if we are drifting into sin, hindered by blind spots, or handicapped by unhelpful leadership styles. Accountability practised well means encouragement and affirmation when we are on right paths, as well as correction when we are on wrong ones. If a congregation thinks the senior pastor or staff team are unaccountable, it will send out subtle signals to that effect. Healthy interaction between leaders and non-leaders can reassure the main body of the church that the former are serious about holiness, and want to conform in private to the image they have in public.

For some church leaders, accountability means praying regularly with a fellow church member, and trying to be honest about what is going on in the church. For others, it might involve meeting someone outside the church, perhaps a leader from another church, and aiming at mutual accountability. According to Martin Saunders, writing in *Christianity* magazine, US research indicates that as many as 50% of Christian men, and 40% of Christian women, battle with an attraction to internet pornography.[5] Such people can help each other through mutual accountability: you can purchase software that will alert someone else to the sites you have visited. There are more subtle addictions for church leaders: they may be driven by a need to succeed, and a desire for the praise of the congregation; this can lead to criticism of other churches, or complaining about the body of their own church membership. There is no computer software for dealing with these things – but like other addictions, they can be damaging to the soul.

1.4 BE AWARE OF 'PROFESSIONAL' MINISTRY PRESSURES

In Mark 10 Jesus makes a stark contrast between how the world's leaders operate, and how He expects His followers to lead. This is one of the very few direct references to leadership in His teaching (though it is underpinned by His instructions on living in the kingdom of God). Jesus had just rebuked James and John for misunderstanding their role in the kingdom, and now he points out that a disciple 'wanting to be great' must be the slave of all:

> *When the ten heard about this, they became indignant with James and John. Jesus called them together and said, 'You know that those who are regarded as rulers of the Gentiles lord it over them, and their high officials exercise authority over them. Not so with you. Instead, whoever wants to become great among you must be your servant, and whoever wants to be first must be slave of all.*

For even the Son of Man did not come to be served, but to serve, and to give his life as a ransom for many.' (Mark 10:41–45)

Peter evidently got the message, because in his own letter he reminded those in leadership:

Be shepherds of God's flock that is under your care, serving as overseers – not because you must, but because you are willing, as God wants you to be; not greedy for money, but eager to serve; not lording it over those entrusted to you, but being examples to the flock. And when the Chief Shepherd appears, you will receive the crown of glory that will never fade away. (1 Peter 5:2–4)

Christian leadership has subtle temptations: the desire to be seen as successful, achieve numerical growth in the church, have ministry plans fulfilled, gain financial security (personally, and for the church), to attain a 'professional' status within the denomination, and to have the approval of the people. Many of these aims can be pursued in the name of 'God's will for our church'. But Jesus, and Peter, are very clear that the servant role must be the primary one for every leader, manifested in how he or she deals with other people: resisting the temptation to manipulate; enabling others to flourish, without being defensive; and being prepared to do the unpleasant tasks.

There is no guarantee that such a disposition will shield a leader from criticism, but if their ministry is modelled on the pattern of Jesus they will help their church to flourish. Such a ministry will set a high standard, and those members who leave in the hope of finding something better elsewhere may well be disappointed.

1.5 DON'T TAKE YOURSELF TOO SERIOUSLY

A good friend of mine believes that you can identify wise leaders by asking two questions about them: do they take God *seriously*, and do they take themselves *non-seriously*? Both questions are important: you would expect any church leader to take God seriously, but the same leader could well take him/herself *too* seriously. As comedian Bob Monkhouse famously said: 'They laughed when I said I wanted to get into comedy. Well, they're not laughing now!' A church leader must see the funny side of life. Church leadership can be an excessive burden if leaders believe too much in their own importance – or in 'getting it right'. Church is important and souls are at stake, but we are called to serve God, not to be the lord of our own universe. Some of Jesus' most severe criticism was reserved for the Pharisees, who were so pernickety about the finer points of the law that they overlooked the joyous revelation of the goodness of God's kingdom. Jesus promises us that if we follow His way we will find abundance and rest:

> 'Come to me, all you who are weary and burdened, and I will give you rest. Take my yoke upon you and learn from me, for I am gentle and humble in heart, and you will find rest for your souls. For my yoke is easy and my burden is light.' (Matthew 11:28–30)

We may see these verses in the context of non-believers needing to come for forgiveness. In fact the word 'yoke' can mean 'the style of interpretation of a Rabbi'. Jesus is saying that His teaching is distinct from the rabbis' teaching, which leaves its hearers soul-weary and over-burdened. If this is our own experience, then maybe we have taken someone else's yoke upon us and are failing to 'learn from' Jesus.

Rick Warren provides helpful advice in a podcast he gave on www.pastors.com: *divert daily* (don't work for the whole day), *withdraw weekly* (enjoy a whole day free from work), and *abandon annually* (take a proper holiday from work). For some Christian leaders, the biggest battle is not with criticism, personal sin, or demonic encounters – but with their diary.

1.6 MAKE THE PURSUIT OF GOD YOUR TOP PRIORITY

In his book *The God Chasers*,[6] Tommy Tenney says: 'The gnawing vacuum of emptiness in the midst of my accomplishments just got worse. I was in a frustrating funk, a divine depression of destiny … I am a fourth-generation Spirit-filled Christian, three generations deep into ministry, but I must be honest with you: I was sick of church … There had to be more. I was desperate for a God encounter (of the closest kind).'

His book has received some criticism: the title itself creates the image of Christians speeding around the world, like archaeologists desperate to find hidden treasure. Even if you're not that kind of Christian, you can agree that Tenney's aim – to know God better – is a good one. A.W. Tozer said that the prayer meeting is the hardest meeting to get Christians to attend, because God is the only attraction; it is also true that Christian leaders find it hard to 'make an appointment' with God – because they are so busy with church work. I am sad to admit that I have sometimes led people in prayer knowing that with my busyness at the start of the day, this is the first time I have spoken with God myself.

In his book *7 Laws of Spiritual Success*[7] Selwyn Hughes, argues that the first law of spiritual success is to make sure that worship has priority in our lives. Selwyn's *Every Day with Jesus* devotional notes were designed to help people spend time with Jesus, and his work continues after his death, with about one million daily readers.

'The pursuit of God' will mean different things to different people: no doubt it means something to you in terms of your church tradition, or your recent experience. It hardly feels appropriate to mention pursuing God in a book about closing the church's back door, for pursuing God should never be a means to an end – we're not saying 'Get close to God, and people will stay in your church'. But if seeking God is our priority, no part of life remains untouched; and this advice is good for every area of Christian life and ministry.

1.7 BE PREPARED TO ADMIT MISTAKES

In *It: How Churches and Leaders can Get It and Keep It*[8] the senior pastor of the multi-campus church 'life.tv', Craig Groeschel, argues that to make progress we must try strategies that might fail – especially in church leadership. He writes:

> *God gave me the great gift of failure early in the ministry. Much of what I tried failed. Our drama ministry fell apart. Our attempt at a choir didn't work. Our first mission trip didn't happen. Our Wednesday Bible study crashed before take-off. Our monthly worship night happened only twice ... Most people don't know how often we failed. One of the things our church is known for is meeting in multiple locations. But our first attempt at a video venue was a disaster. After struggling for four months we pulled*

the plug. Three years ago we attempted two out-of-state campuses in the Phoenix area [Groeschel is based in Oklahoma]. It was a matter of months before we realized neither would survive. We were totally embarrassed. Not only did our whole church know about our failure, but so did many other church leaders who were watching. Even worse, we felt horrible about all the money we blew. It was God's money.[9]

Of all the places in the world where we should be able to say 'Sorry, we made a mistake', the church should be top of the list. But it seems that many church leaders are reluctant to admit their mistakes, fearful perhaps that they may lose the confidence of the membership – but their confidence would actually rise if the leaders only had the humility to admit what is already obvious: they are fallible human beings. Admitting failure builds a sense of trust, knowing that we are all working together, facing the same struggle, and seeking by God's help to make progress.

Groeschel argues that it is important to be 'real' about a failure, without pretending it didn't happen or trying to put a good spin on it. This is generally true, though there may be good reasons why a leader might not share everything with a congregation: perhaps there are other parties involved, or there may be unhelpful consequences if information is shared too soon. But hiding mistakes, or pretending all is well when it isn't, is deceitful, and helps no one.

1.8 Never forget that people who come to church are volunteers

When Bill Clinton was president of the United States and seeking counsel from Christian leaders following his affair with White House intern Monica Lewinski, Bill Hybels, senior pastor of Willow Creek Community Church, used to visit him in Washington DC. Hybels recalls how he joked with Clinton that his role as senior pastor was harder than Bill's as the head of the world's greatest superpower – because Clinton could easily fire a staff member who didn't obey his orders: but with church leaders, if they are disliked then people just leave the church![10]

Church leaders are wise to heed Bill Hybels' comment. It doesn't mean they need be any less bold in their leadership, but the ordinary church member doesn't live a life focused on the church like the pastor does; any pastor who forgets that is asking for trouble. This means that church leadership has a distinctly different feel from other kinds of leadership. The senior pastor is not the managing director of 'God's Church plc', but the shepherd of a flock of sheep who need care and nurture, leading and teaching.

1.9 KNOW THE SPECIFIC NEEDS OF YOUR MEMBERSHIP

If you were in a church in a mining village in the 1980s, or a market town during the 'mad cow disease' crisis of 1996, then the socio-economic aspect of church life would have stared you in the face. In the UK the late 1980s saw mines closed and a stand-off between the government and the miners' union, and in 1996 many farms were affected when a strain of CJD infected some cattle, and the government chose to cull many thousands more as a safety precaution. The socio-economic dimensions of church life cannot be ignored. They affect the finances of the church, the focus of pastoral care, and the sorts of topics which are appropriate for Sunday sermons; and a leader's inability to deal with such issues might cause people to leave.

It is not difficult to find out the socio-economic category of the area local to your church. Websites have done all the work for you: see http://www.statistics.gov.uk. A church leader I met on a CWR course told me that checking the socio-economic background of his church was one of his first tasks when assigned to his parish, and that his findings were a big surprise to the stalwarts who had attended the church all their lives. It is good to know how distinct your congregation may be from the local community, and to find out how many members are in work, the sort of jobs they do, the number out of work, and how many live on their own. How can you better serve that community, assisting not only those in your congregation, but also those not yet with you?

1.10 INVITE TRUSTED EXTERNAL LEADERS TO EVALUATE YOUR CHURCH

The Anglicans and Catholics have bishops, Baptists and Methodists have superintendents, and some charismatics have 'apostolic' leaders. Healthy churches can find individuals who are not part of the congregation and can give an objective overview, assessing how the church is progressing, given its particular characteristics, state of leadership and recent history. This may happen formally within a denominational structure, or informally as the church leaders spend time with a respected external advisor. Many churches can thrive for a time without such an audit, but independent advisors provide much-needed evaluation, preventing what has been called 'the idiosyncrasy of independency': churches may think they know what matters, but seen alongside other moves of God in the town or nation they may be 'out on a limb'. A good advisor can prevent a church from going down unfruitful pathways which alienate members and cause them to 'jump ship'.

So a great response to back-door loss is to invite someone to appraise your church, and advise you on the best response. If you find it too awkward to invite someone formally linked with the church, then use an external church leader whom you respect, or someone who specialises in consulting with churches.

2. Values

There are many values that will enhance your church. Values are the unspoken norms determining that things are done well; they flow from both our doctrinal beliefs and our understanding of God and humanity. The values identified here are specifically related to 'back-door loss', though there may be others that apply to your own church.

2.1 ENCOURAGE PRAYER FOR YOUR LEADERS

In Colossians 4 the apostle Paul specifically asks the church to pray for him so that he may proclaim the gospel message clearly. Paul was writing from prison, and this may seem a strange prayer request given that he had one of the finest minds the Church has ever known. But the verse is a reminder that we need prayer even for our strong qualities: and if Paul needed prayer, so do our church leaders today.

You will have noticed that many of the reasons for 'back-door loss' stem from church leadership. Leaders play a key role in determining what may or may not happen in their church, and to some extent they set the 'spiritual temperature'. Leaders who are Spirit-filled and energetic for God's purpose, working with their gifts, play an essential role. In the Old Testament, God judges the nation by the quality of a king's walk with Him; and though the

New Testament concept of leadership is not identical, being seen as typically plural in the local church – Acts 14:23 and 20:17, 28, Philippians 1:1, Titus 1:5 and James 5:14 all speak of 'elders', ie more than one leader – there is no doubting the significance of a leader in the church.

If you are a leader, you are wise to ask for prayer – of fellow leaders, and the congregation as a whole. A church that prays for its leaders will be less likely to have members leave because of the leadership. There will be a greater sense of respect for those who lead, and an awareness that as the members pray, they are enabling God to aid and equip the leaders. If a member believes the leadership is weak but prays for them regularly, the member may well find that God brings change in the way they hoped! And if the member still feels they should leave, at least it won't be on a whim.

2.2 DEVELOP HEALTHY RELATIONSHIPS

The apostle Peter tells us that 'love covers over a multitude of sins' (1 Pet. 4:8). We could add that love covers a multitude of reasons why people leave the church. The giving and receiving of genuine love in a congregation is essential for oiling the wheels of fellowship. But true love can only be given and received when we know one another. We have already noted that our modern forms of church are different from the smaller communities that typically prevailed in the first century of the Church, when the New Testament was being written. In those days many believers faced persecution for their faith, so didn't just *want*, but *needed*, to be with other believers. Today, too, what believers share in the worship community makes it distinct from every other gathering in their life, and a key source of support.

We have already noted that it is possible to be a spectator in church. This may be valuable if the member needs space to listen and worship in their own time; but in the long term, people who do not 'connect' with others are prone to moving on if they discover they don't like some aspect of the church's life.

2.3 VALUE INDIVIDUALITY

In his bestselling academic book, *Metaphors We Live By*,[11] George Lakoff argues that our mental images of life are often more powerful than reality. The application of biblical images, in the wrong hands, has done the Church a disservice. The metaphor of the body was used by the apostle Paul to explain that church members are interdependent, and one in Christ. No part of the body can pretend that it doesn't need the others, so no one can claim that their gift is more important than anyone else's. It's a great picture. The trouble is that some have extended the metaphor too far, and assumed that the church's progress has to be 'as a body', with everyone sharing a specific common vision, moving in the same direction and arriving at the same place – rather like a group of walkers going for a ramble. The word 'specific' is important. The leaders we are concerned with would say that as a church body we must all follow one calling, without considering the different ways in which church members are led by the Spirit. Ironically, such blinkered leaders have misunderstood Paul's body metaphor, and are acting as if their gift of leadership (if they are so gifted) is more significant than anyone else's. Their attitude is: 'Listen to me, and I will tell you where to go!'

The irony is that this approach alienates those whom every church leader would give their right arm for (to use a more modern body image). People with drive and enthusiasm for God's work can find that when their church has a single, exclusive focus, they are left feeling sad, frustrated or discouraged.

If your church has a specific vision, or a written 'mission statement', it is important to ensure it is broad enough to include people whom God has tapped on the shoulder, and told: 'Do this.' If they think you don't care about their call, they may leave.

2.4 DEAL CONSTRUCTIVELY WITH CONFLICT

In *Metaphors We Live By*, George Lakoff writes of the many times in which we may use military metaphors to emphasise the importance of a situation. Chelsea vs Manchester United is 'the Battle of the Bridge' (Chelsea play at Stamford Bridge) – but it's just a game of football! Military metaphors litter our conversations: 'Your claims are indefensible'; 'He attacked every point in my argument'; 'I have lots of ammunition in my arsenal'; 'His criticisms were right on target'; 'I demolished his case'; 'If you use that strategy, she'll wipe you out.' Lakoff's point is that military metaphors create a style of conversation that can be unnecessarily confrontational or aggressive.

The church can be the same. Sadly it's not just the hymn *Onward, Christian Soldiers* that uses militaristic language. Leaders think in terms of 'winning' and 'losing' their argument, their 'fight' for the kingdom, being in the midst of 'the battle'. And I write this as an employee of CWR, whose initials originally meant 'Crusade for World Revival'!

I recall chatting with one pastor who spoke of the 'time bombs' left by a previous incumbent: he could, instead, have described issues that had been 'swept under the carpet', and were bound to be seen at some point in the future. Language affects attitudes: it takes a wise leader to know when a problem needs dealing with forcefully, or whether intervention might make matters worse. Perhaps the problem would have resolved itself. It isn't always easy for a leader to know whether to get involved, and if confrontation follows they might ask: why didn't I stay out of it?

Conflict is not always inevitable. A leader can acquire a tender touch, and learn how to 'disagree agreeably': then there is less confrontation, and more mutual acceptance. A church can arrange sessions on conflict management, perhaps led by an outsider who is skilled at the task; this can help leaders prepare for the inevitable conflicts that will come their way. Too often, an 'expert' is called in when it is too late, and people have been alienated.

2.5 PEOPLE BEFORE PROGRAMMES

For some leaders, the main focus is implementing church programmes to meet aims x, y and z – regardless of whether these aims are on the heart of the members. We saw earlier that this is a downside of the move for every church to have a 'mission statement' or 'vision statement'. A vision can be great if it helps clarify where the church, as a group, is heading, but deadly if it alienates those in the congregation who do not share this particular vision. It is surely much wiser to have a broad, encompassing mission that every member can play a part in.

The New Testament gives relatively little space to programmes.[12] The letters of Paul contain almost no guidance for accomplishing ministry goals, or ways of meeting the needs of particular groups within the church. That is not to suggest that Paul himself was without strategies: he clearly uses wise approaches in his work, as recorded in Acts, seeking to spread the good news of Christ across the Roman Empire; but his main aim seems to be helping people learn and grow in Christ, rather than using particular techniques. Today, our mega-churches and mini-churches and all-sorts-of-size churches can use a variety of programmes for ministry. I recall my time in a sizeable church where we had ministries for youth, children, old people, street people, students, international students, mums and toddlers, and business people. I don't believe we were wrong to set up teams to deliver this range of ministries. But a problem may arise when 'the good' becomes the enemy of 'the best', and the implementation of these good programmes takes priority over the individuals in the church. We may be forcing round pegs into square holes for the sake of 'the programme'. Church members may be giving all their free time to running programmes, and have precious little time for anything else – including their own needs.

2.6 Work with your people

My first church boss used a saying from the world of politics to describe church leadership – an 1867 quote from the Prussian politician Otto von Bismarck: 'Politics is the art of the possible'!

A wise leader learns to take people on a journey of change at the right pace and with appropriate consultation. It is indeed 'the art of the possible': although we believe in a God of the impossible, we have to work at any given time within the limits of people's state of mind and heart. After all, isn't this how God works with us? Of course we pray for change, and above all change in *people*: church programmes cannot be as calculated or mechanistic as a factory system producing widgets. So although church leaders may be greatly tempted to court confrontation when the church seems unwilling to move, it is wiser for the leader to work with the congregation; leave confrontation for those rare occasions when God clearly leads you to confront and it would be disobedient to do otherwise.

James Thwaites, author of *Church that Works*,[13] was the pastor of a large church in Australia, and in a memorable sermon he pointed out that many in the congregation didn't actually want to be there. He said he was grateful for their commitment, but felt his role as a pastor was to 'stir them up' to go forward with God. He suggested that if they didn't want to attend church, they should stay away and ask God what they should do instead – and that if he as pastor could support them in their seeking, he would be happy to do so. It should be added that this challenge didn't come completely out of the blue, and many members went on to start 'churches' elsewhere, notably in their workplaces – just as Thwaites had hoped they might.

Such a call may seem radical, but it demonstrates that God may already be at work within church members. Their leaders need to work with them, rather than set the church on a course that is about their own dreams, rather than God's plans.

3. Communication

3.1 KEEP COMMUNICATION CHANNELS OPEN IN THE CHURCH

When the mood of a church is that 'the leaders are just not listening', this may be literally true. Not listening can mean 'not doing what I think they should do', but it can also mean that the people do not feel they have the ear of the leaders. Church members like to know that they have been heard, even if their views are at odds with those of the leaders. In some churches I have attended, you felt that you needed to have a major crisis to get any time with a leader.

Churches can overcome this problem in various ways. Some hold an 'open forum' where questions can be directed to the leadership. Other churches allow anyone to speak to the pastor or vicar after particular services. Some set aside a time in the week when the staff are available to anyone. But the ideal is regular contact between the leadership and the congregation, with no set agenda. It has been said that the biblical view of leadership is based on a rabbinic principle whereby leaders and followers work closely together, so church leaders should spend 'significant time' with members. On this view, you only have 'true elders' when you have a 'true church' – with gatherings that are small enough for good communication. Certainly, some system needs to be in place for leaders to hear what members are saying, both formally and informally.

3.2 TEACH PEOPLE HOW TO COMMUNICATE

When you discover the real reasons why some people leave a church, they may seem trivial. The leader asks, was that really the trigger for a whole family to change their place of worship? It is seldom a particular event in itself, but its *perception*. Our perception is caused by our beliefs, and our beliefs may be formed by lies, from our own hearts or from other people – lies which we choose to believe. To take a simple example, Fred may be upset because the senior pastor 'blanked' him in the street: he walked straight past, without greeting him. The next Sunday, this same pastor has occasion to reprimand Fred's children for their silly behaviour. Fred begins to think: 'The pastor is targeting me.' An uneasiness develops. Now Fred is negative towards the pastor because of his hurt feelings, and he makes negative comments to others, whom he knows have doubts about the pastor. Now a number of church members, not just Fred, are negative towards the pastor. The truth of the matter is that the senior pastor was lost in thought in the street, anticipating a funeral he was about to conduct, when Fred passed him. He simply didn't notice Fred. And the pastor reprimanded Fred's children along with a number of others, though Fred's children reported that 'the pastor told us off this morning' without mentioning the other children involved.

The pastor had no problem with Fred at all. But Fred *perceived* that he had. Fred's belief that the pastor was targeting him was based on a lie, which he chose to believe.

When you multiply this sort of scenario over time, and with a large group of church people, you realise the vast potential for misunderstandings which lead to grievances. It is no surprise therefore to discover that in the New Testament there is much teaching against negative speech, especially gossip. Indeed, gossip and slander are given higher priority than other sins in New Testament lists – Romans 1:29–31, for example: 'They have become filled with every kind of wickedness, evil, greed and depravity. They are full of envy, murder, strife, deceit and malice. They are gossips, slanderers, God-haters, insolent, arrogant and boastful; they invent ways of doing evil; they disobey their parents; they are senseless, faithless, heartless, ruthless.'

So, however people like to dress up their reason for leaving the church, sometimes the root of it all is plain and simple: sin, in the form of gossip or slander, has infected their judgment about individuals, and the consequent rift has not been healed.

Helping church members avoid the dangers of expressing opinions inappropriately, and of a 'gossip mentality', can be a major way of tackling back-door losses. We had a friend who taught us to resolutely refuse to listen to gossip. He would ask, 'Is this first-hand information?' If the answer was 'No', then he would say, 'I don't want to know.' Gossip is the passing on of information when we are neither part of the problem, nor part of the solution. Stamp out gossip and you stamp out much church conflict, and the reason many members leave.

3.3 LET YOUR PEOPLE KNOW THAT YOU ARE INTERESTED

Wise church leaders will find ways in which those not confident enough to approach a leader, or stand up in a meeting, can make their views known. This may mean soliciting views one-to-one from the more quiet and timid individuals, perhaps at an informal church event where conversation is relaxed. When there is a major issue up for discussion it is so easy for people to hear what they want to hear, or misunderstand what is being said. Their fear of the implications of what they 'hear' can colour their view, so that what they end up believing is some distance from what was actually said! So small-group discussions are invaluable, as are one-to-one conversations where people can voice their concerns, and leaders can respond appropriately – and correct misunderstandings. One church spent a whole weekend handing over the reins of leadership from the senior leader to the 'understudy'. The senior leader had founded the church, so there was a lot of adjustment to make, and some pain expressed in the workshops and open sessions during the weekend. But the process was massively useful. Members felt their views had been heard, and they were more able to get behind the new leader.

3.4 COMMUNICATE YOUR PLANS WELL

The senior leader in a church needs to spend as long communicating the church's vision as he or she does preaching the sermon. How should the vision be presented? What might the objections be? What is the time-scale? What is clear? What isn't clear? As a rule of thumb, leaders say that you need to communicate the vision so often that you as a leader become sick of it – and then carry on communicating it! Leaders see what followers cannot see, and so the latter need to be persuaded and convinced. Sometimes the need that is raised is self-evident: for example, our church is falling down and needs rebuilding. But other church needs are less concrete (forgive the pun). Starting a costly ministry to a sector of society that no one is reaching, investing heavily in more staff, changing the style of services to be more open to non-believers – all these are initiatives that members might not like. And because they are complex, they invite opposition – the 'if you do that, this will happen' argument. So communication is vital: clear, perhaps with a Powerpoint-type visual presentation, written, oral, careful, timely, and repeated. The leader can say at the end: 'Got it?'

3.5 DON'T IGNORE THE 'UNOFFICIAL' LEADERS

If you are planning major changes or initiatives, then pay special attention to communicating with the 'unofficial leadership'. In the past, the official church leaders have agreed on a direction, only to have it undermined by the holders of unofficial power. This does not imply that we should bow to their wishes. It simply means that providing information, and discussing with each individual informally, can bypass future difficulties. Once members understand your proposal, and its probable outcome, they are more likely to become your allies. I have known situations where the church has a former pastor worshipping with it (either from that church, or a neighbouring church). This can be intimidating for the current incumbent, but the 'official leader' would be wise to check out where these 'unofficial leaders' stand on major decisions. Similarly, 'church stalwarts', whose longevity in the church is known and appreciated, need to be treated carefully. Whether these people deserve to be unofficial leaders is beside the point. If church members look to them for a lead, whoever is the 'official leader', then their support for your plans is crucial.

4. Congregational priorities

4.1 FOCUS ON SEEKING GOD'S PRESENCE IN YOUR GATHERINGS

In the past I have been a keen supporter of the 'seeker-driven churches' movement. This has helped many to see that outmoded church systems and practices needed to be ditched if non-believers are to hear the message of Jesus. But there is a dimension to public worship that can be forgotten within seeker-driven approaches. It is hinted at in the early chapters of Acts where, after the judgment of God fell on Ananias and Sapphira for lying to the Holy Spirit, we learn: 'The apostles performed many miraculous signs and wonders among the people. And all the believers used to meet together in Solomon's Colonnade. No-one else dared join them, even though they were highly regarded by the people. Nevertheless, more and more men and women believed in the Lord and were added to their number' (Acts 5:12–14).

People were both attracted to, and repelled by, the Church in Acts. There is something about a people who know and trust and worship God that will attract those who are spiritually hungry, and alienate those who prefer to live their life without God. 'Seeker services' can focus on the programme, without trying to discover the 'felt presence' of God in the gathering. The apostle Paul wrote: 'My message and my preaching were not with wise and persuasive words, but with a demonstration of the Spirit's power, so that your faith might not rest on men's wisdom, but on God's power' (1 Cor. 2:4–5). It seems that God acts in such a way that hearers know He is present.

Jonathan Edwards wrote during a time of 'refreshing' which came to the churches he pastored in New England in the 1730s. He put it like this:

> *But, if there is indeed a power entirely different from and beyond our power, or the power of means, then certainly it is in no wise unreasonable to suppose that this effect should very frequently be produced as to make it very manifest and sensible that it is so. Why is it unreasonable to suppose it should seem to be so, to them who are the subjects of it? If persons tell of effects that seem to them not to be from the natural power or operation of their minds, but from the supernatural powers of some other agent, should it at once be looked upon as a sure evidence of their being under a delusion because things seem to them to be as they are?*[14]

The language may sound archaic, but the acknowledgement of the difference that God makes is clear. When all is said and done, the sense of God's presence in a church has a powerful effect on those who gather, and this is important in any analysis of why people leave the church. In some cases, as Luke points out in Acts 5:13, the presence of God is not welcomed by members. But any church where people leave because God is manifestly present, really has something more serious to worry about than a back-door problem!

4.2 ENSURE SMALL GROUPS HELP RATHER THAN HINDER CHURCH DEVELOPMENT

Having been in church leadership myself, I know it is easy to think that a simple division into small groups, arranged geographically or in some other way, is the best way of organising the church. But there are two problems with this: the first concerns the way we gather, and the second why we gather.

Firstly, concerning the way we gather: people are not sheep, even though

Scripture commonly uses the metaphor. Home groups based on arbitrary selection have worked, but they often feel very artificial. When small groups are formed, the members should have some choice. In a church Ron attended, group leaders' names were put on a notice-board and individuals were given the opportunity to sign up. This meant that some who thought the named persons would be suitable leaders soon discovered they weren't – but the big advantage was that more church members signed up than previously, because they appreciated having a choice.

Fundamentally, however, we need to analyse why church members come together. The commonly held view, 'we get together for fellowship', needs unpacking. 'Fellowship' is one of those key Christian words that is rarely defined. It literally means 'having a share with someone in something'. It is true that the basis for any small-group church fellowship is to 'share in' Christ, and we would certainly not question that. However, having observed and participated in dozens of small groups across a range of churches, it is our experience that many small groups lack dynamism because they have unrealistic or inappropriate aims.

Many small church groups are in truth a means whereby the church leaders aim to meet the pastoral needs of the church – an especially vital function if the church is larger than about a hundred, or the lead pastor is not strong in the pastoral area. So members will gather in groups, typically for prayer and Bible study, perhaps also for praise and worship, and to discuss topics raised in the Sunday services. There is nothing wrong with all these group functions, but there is a better way.

Why not have a variety of small groups, some based on the multi-purpose model described above, but others which have a single common purpose? This may be short-term – studying a pertinent topic, such as 'debt' or parenting, or divorce recovery, or sharing our faith, or 'holiness'. Or it may be a group set up with a specific purpose, for example to serve the elderly – gardening, decorating, shopping, and so on. Or it may be a group with a common interest – playing a sport like badminton, or pursuing an activity like sewing or knitting. Time spent together in such single-purpose groups would be seen as valuable: sharing in the group's activity would be a means of building relationships, perhaps with times of prayer introduced as appropriate. Such a group experience would be new to some members, not because the activities themselves are unusual (many churches do these things), but because they would provide a special 'small-group experience'. In our view such groups would fulfil God's purposes for the church every bit as much as the classic, geographically arranged Bible study/prayer group. The beauty of these single-focus groups is that they have a short-term life, so that those joining don't feel they will be in the group for too long.

We have elaborated on this concept because the small-group experience provides the spiritual glue that helps a church community to grow, through the inspiration of the Holy Spirit; and such groups help to develop genuine relationships into which church members enter voluntarily. Such supportive relationships offset the normal ups and downs of life experienced by all members, and such relationship-building discourages a 'back-door problem' in the church.

4.3 GET AN 'OUTSIDE CHURCH' LIFE

Small groups are not everyone's cup of tea, so why not experiment with other ways of encouraging fellowship? Church picnics, meals, 'open house', are all excellent gatherings for helping people on the fringe to become integrated.

More important than small groups and church gatherings, however, is the creation of a culture that gives permission to church members *not* to devote all their free time to the church. Some church members spend an alarming amount of time on church activities. I am not suggesting that a leader should keep a timesheet on members, or an electronic tag to monitor the time they spend on church premises (and I hope that doesn't give 'control freak' pastors any ideas!). But the point is that over-commitment means church people have less time for the unstructured, relaxed relationships which are vital if a sense of internal fellowship is to blossom – and if church members are to relate well with outsiders who don't know 'the songs of Zion'. To put it succinctly: 'think people, not programmes'.

4.4 BE ALERT TO THE FRINGES OF THE CHURCH

A healthy church has a fringe, ie a group of people who are on the periphery: attending services and meetings, perhaps only occasionally, but not yet involved as church members.

In his book *Purpose Driven Church*,[15] Rick Warren distinguishes between different groups which church leaders need to be aware of: the community, the crowd, the congregation, the committed, and the core. He draws a series of concentric circles to represent each group. The *community* are those outside the church – the non-believers, and believers who are in nearby churches or know people in the church. The *crowd* are those who gather from time to time, the *congregation* are the regular members, the *committed* are the maturing members, and the *core* are the leaders: lay and ordained ministers of the church.

Most of today's church members were probably on the fringe (part of the crowd) at one time. If you find that people on the fringe never get involved, that will tell you something. Is there a communication issue (they don't know what the church is about)? Is it a commitment issue (they feel the church is too 'high-pressure' spiritually for them)? Is it a building issue (they think the church premises are too small or unattractive)? And remember, the reasons people don't join the church may overlap with the reasons why they leave.

4.5 INCLUDE YOUNG PEOPLE IN THE LIFE OF THE CHURCH

I recall an older person in the church I grew up in, saying that the young people needed looking after because they were 'the church of the future'. I am sure he was well-meaning, and as a young person at the time I was impressed by his foresight. But his attitude signalled a problem that many churches face. If the young people are 'the church of the future', what is the present church made up of? Where do the children and young people feature now? If young people don't feel they and their contribution are important, they may find integration into church difficult later on. Separate activities for young people may be appropriate, but beware of creating an alternative 'children's church' divorced from the life of the main church. Services should include input from young people from time to time, and if the preacher's sermon topics are relevant to the lives of all hearers, young people will form a 'mental map' and realise that they are also included. Today church leaders face unprecedented challenges, so it won't be easy. But young people are part of today's Church – and they must be integrated in churches today, if there is to be a Church of tomorrow.

4.6 CELEBRATE THE 'RITES OF PASSAGE'

In the past, reaching the age of 21 meant you had gained a 'key to the door of the house'. Today, 21 is less significant than 18 – but even 18 is not that special. By then, a young person has already passed a number of key ages, as the following milestones in the context of the UK show.

At 10 you have reached the age of criminal responsibility. This means that you can be convicted of a criminal offence.

At 13 you can have a part-time job.

At 14 you are considered legally responsible for your actions, so if you commit a criminal offence you will be treated the same as an adult (except for sentencing). You can enter a pub, though you can't buy or drink alcohol there.

At 16 you can have a full-time job if you have left school. You can get married with your parents' or guardians' consent. You can ride a 50cc moped. At 16 a girl can legally have sex with a boy, and she can have an abortion without her parents' consent. You can drink alcohol with a meal in a restaurant or the eating area of a pub.

At 17 you can hold a licence to drive most vehicles. You can pilot a plane. You can emigrate. A care order can no longer be made on you.

At 18 you are seen as an adult in the eyes of the law. You can vote in general elections, make a will, and die for your country. You can place a bet, have a tattoo and buy fireworks.[16]

In some faiths, age is a key signal of a person's welcome into the next stage of worship, and this applies in some churches too. But for most churches, the celebration of a 'rite of passage' is a private family affair. Integrating young people into the church might be easier if the church found appropriate ways of celebrating key stages in young people's lives. At what point does the church leadership have different expectations of its young people? When might they be consulted as adults, and not merely as 'the youth'? If they were treated as adults, would this help the church to keep them later, when they are tempted to drift away? Maybe young people need to be reminded that they are part of the church too, to be initiated appropriately, and helped to move on to the next level in their walk with God.

4.7 DEVELOP A CONSTRUCTIVE PROCESS FOR RELEASING PEOPLE WHO CHOOSE TO LEAVE

We have noted that you may not know why an individual or family have left, so it can be useful to implement a process for when people do leave. Jobs have 'exit interviews' so that human resources managers can learn from outgoing employees. It would be useful if the church leadership had similar conversations with those who are leaving. Of course, such a dialogue can only be voluntary, but it would help both parties. The church will know why they left and the individual or family can be cared for pastorally at the time of leaving, and perhaps advised about other churches to join. It may be appropriate for the church leader to 'introduce' the leavers to a new church leader. When Andy was in pastoral ministry, his church leaders would have conversations with other church ministers in the area, when their members moved on or when other people came to them.

A 'leaving conversation' can help things to end well. When my wife and I had to change churches, to attend a church closer to where we had moved to, it was good to have a chat with the pastor of the church we were part of, who was able to bless us as we left. Sometimes those leaving feel embarrassed, assuming that they will be out of favour with the pastor, when the opposite is true. As a good pastor friend of mine used to say: 'I would rather they went on with God somewhere else, than backslide here!'

4.8 KNOW AND TEACH GOD'S 'BIG STORY'

There's a story about a traveller who came upon three individuals working with stone. Curious to know what they were doing, he asked the first, 'What are you doing with these stones?' Without hesitation the worker replied, 'I am a stone cutter, and I am cutting stones.' Not satisfied with this answer, the traveller approached the second worker and asked, 'What are you doing with these stones?' The second worker paused for a moment and then explained, 'I am a stone cutter, and I am earning money to support my family.' Having had two different answers to the same question, the traveller asked the third worker, 'What are you doing with these stones?' The man stopped what he was doing, bringing his chisel to his side. Deep in thought, the worker gazed at the traveller and spoke these words: 'I am a stone cutter, and I am building a cathedral!'

The story is often used to demonstrate the importance of *vision*, and it can be applied to various aspects of church life to show that vision is crucial. Members need a vision of how their church fits into God's overall purposes. Church members can feel they are ploughing a lone furrow in a small corner of the UK, or they can see themselves enacting God's ongoing purposes to restore this planet, His creation.

In recent years, there have been various approaches to understanding God's story. My CWR colleague, Philip Greenslade, wrote *A Passion for God's Story*,[17] and runs courses at CWR helping church people understand how the Bible narrative works, and how their church can be seen to fit into God's purposes. Tom Wright, Bishop of Durham, sees the Bible in five Acts: Act 1 Creation; Act 2 Fall; Act 3 Israel falls; Act 4 Jesus; Act 5 The Church. Tom writes:

> *Those who live in this fifth act have an ambiguous relationship with the four previous acts, not because they are being disloyal to them but precisely because they are being loyal to them as part of the story. If someone in the fifth act of* All's Well that Ends Well *were to start repeating speeches from earlier acts, instead of those which belonged to the fifth act itself, the whole play would begin to unravel. We must act in the appropriate manner for this moment in the story; this will be in direct continuity with previous acts … but such continuity also implies discontinuity, a moment where genuinely new things can and do happen.*[18]

Tom Wright goes on to explain that we have the responsibility, as people of the fifth act, to 'improvise' in response to the four previous acts:

> *The notion of 'improvising' is important, but sometimes misunderstood. As all musicians know, improvisation does not at all mean a free-for-all where 'anything goes', but precisely a disciplined and careful listening to all the other voices around us, and a constant attention to the themes, rhythms and harmonies of the complete performance so far, the performance we are now called to continue. At the same time, of course, it invites us, while being fully obedient to the music so far, and fully attentive to the voices around us, to explore fresh expressions, provided they will eventually lead to that ultimate resolution which appears in the New Testament as the goal, the full and complete new creation which was gloriously anticipated in Jesus' resurrection. The music so far, the voices around us, and the ultimate multi-part harmony of God's new world: these, taken together, form the parameters for appropriate improvisation in the reading of Scripture and the announcement and living out of the*

gospel it contains. All Christians, all churches, are free to improvise their own variations designed to take the music forwards. No Christian, no church, is free to play out of tune.[19]

Seeing the 'big picture' in this way helps church leaders and members alike to realise that their work joins with that of Christians down through the centuries who have seen a faithful God accomplishing His purposes, and that we are part of God's continuing drama. If a church ignores or underplays their own part they are likely to get too involved in the tiny dramas of church life, imagining that their church is something else (a museum perhaps!), or that they are involved in something totally disconnected from the purposes of God revealed in Scripture.

However, there is no guarantee that explaining God's 'big picture' to church people will ensure that they want to participate. Some may leave anyway. If they 'bow out' because they have grasped what God is doing and don't want to be part of it, at least you know that they are leaving with some awareness of what God is about.

5. Assessing what you can do

Our look at what we can do to solve the back-door problem may have been frustrating for you, if you feel you have no power to change anything. Stephen Covey, in his bestselling book *Seven Habits of Highly Effective People*,[20] helpfully distinguishes between levels of *concern* and levels of *influence*. For example, you may be concerned about the damage being done to the environment, but aware that reducing your own carbon emissions and recycling waste will have little effect if governments do not meet national targets for these strategies. In this context, you have *high concern* but *low influence*.

Similarly, you may have little concern about your personal appearance – it matters little to you how you look, but unless you are in prison or still dependent on your parents for clothes, you have a high degree of influence over what you wear. In this context, you have *low concern* but *high influence*.

Before you start fretting about the state of your church, it is useful to assess your level of influence. If you are a church leader, like many who attended our 'Closing the Back Door of the Church' courses, you will be able to translate your concern into action. But if you aren't a leader, you may have a lot of concern (you are reading a book about it), but relatively little influence. This can cause extreme frustration, and we have met many church people who are keen to see change but have little opportunity to effect it.

5.1 PRAYER

Perhaps the obvious thing to note first is that you *can* pray – anyone and everyone can! Pray about whether your assessment of the situation is correct. Ask God for insight into the life of your church so that you can see it as He might. Pray for the leaders who have responsibility for leading your church. It's a demanding role, and they may be facing issues that you know nothing about.

5.2 TALK

You can chat with the leaders about your observations. Be calm and clear, always open to being wrong and willing to be corrected. Maybe they have been too busy in other areas of church life to notice what you have seen. Or perhaps they see what you see, but have chosen to focus on other issues.

5.3 CONSIDER

There will come a point when you know whether church life is going to improve, and you must decide what you are prepared to live with. Maybe you can be content in having sought to bring change from a position of non-influence. Perhaps you will have to wait until God gives you greater direct influence on the congregation. Meanwhile, you can continue to pray. Certainly it is not helpful for you, or other church members, to moan and grumble, or to speak ill of the leaders.

If you are a leader, you can accomplish some changes easily, but if you are wise you will know that bigger changes take time, and cannot be rushed. In business there is a clear management structure, and lines of authority. The managing director can make a decision on Monday, and implement change on Tuesday. A church is different. Most of the 'team' is voluntary. They don't spend nearly as long together as co-workers in a business environment, and there must be a winning of hearts and minds, which often takes longer than we think.

6. Is it all over?

When I was working for *Christianity* magazine I wrote two articles on when it is right to close a church. It wasn't the most popular two-part series, and one reader wrote in enraged at the editor's 'negativity' in printing the articles. They made it clear that there are times when, for whatever reason, God's kingdom purposes are better served if a church's members move elsewhere, or merge with another congregation. The possibility of closure also needs to be raised in this book. Sometimes it is necessary to lock the doors and throw away the key.

Ron writes: 'There is a season when closure is appropriate. Some years ago I was reading about a church that was holding its very last service. It could have been gloomy, but actually it was an occasion for great celebration. This was an inner-city church in America, and the congregation had just grown old. They felt it was time to close, but they refused to see closure as a sad event. The church's leaders had planted eleven other churches, and in the following years they planted eleven more. So this was a time to give thanks for an ending, and to celebrate new beginnings. I think there is a season for closure, a time for old things to stop and new things to start. There will be a time for your ministry, and mine, to end. Then, God will raise up another way or another person. We have to hold our ministry lightly in our hands.'

If closure is the necessary course of action, I am sure it won't be done lightly and without prayer. But it can be done celebrating the past and looking forward to what can be accomplished in the future. If God opens up new areas of service for you and others in the church, you will be glad you had the courage to act, rather than let things drag on past their time.

Questions for discussion

1. Are you concerned about declining numbers in your church? If so, what factors concern you?
2. Are your church leaders aware of the challenges facing the local church, and the global Church?
3. Do you think the people who attend your church have a clear understanding of Jesus' teaching about the qualities and lifestyle of a disciple?

4. In your experience, have any of the strategies suggested in this chapter been tried? What were the factors leading to their success or failure?

WHY PEOPLE LEAVE 'THE CHURCH'

Most people who have left your church will wind up somewhere else. But some may not just leave your church, but 'the Church' as a whole. Research suggests that this is not a homogeneous group: some remain enthusiastic followers of Jesus; others have a period of reflection before returning to a different church; and many, sadly, abandon the Church and the Christian faith altogether.[1]

In this chapter we will consider some of the factors that cause folk to leave the Church. These are typically factors that church leaders can do nothing about, though as we shall see in Chapter 5, leaders can make some adjustments to mitigate their effects.

The factors we are looking at largely affect Western Christians, living in countries which are called 'post-Christian', ie where there is a heritage of Christian values which, though lingering and affecting many, no longer have a pervasive influence on the whole culture. This discussion relates specifically to Christians in the UK, but we hope it is relevant to you if your country and culture are different.

1. A poor local expression of 'the Church'

Many people leave 'the' Church because of their experience of 'a' church. For some it was a one-off attendance, while others went for a long period, perhaps during their school or teenage years. They allowed themselves to believe the crazy notion that because that one church wasn't what they were looking for, they should leave the Church because all churches were the same. My suspicion is that in truth, they knew that another church would be different – they probably attended the odd wedding, christening and funeral – but so negative was their experience, they were unwilling to give another church the benefit of the doubt. This is like someone who has a lifelong phobia of dentists because of a painful childhood experience of one dentist.

We need to be clear that such a person may not be leaving 'the faith' as such, or that they may have never come to faith at all. They have perhaps become inoculated from real faith, rather as schoolchildren dismiss Christianity because their only sniff of it came in hearing the head teacher misquote the Bible to make a moralistic point in school assembly.

You will no doubt have a view about whether or not certain churches are poor local expressions of the Church. Certainly in the West, the decline of spiritual life in many fellowships is such that the word 'church' describes its past rather than its present: it may once have been a gathering of people who named Jesus as Lord, but the days when they were a genuine 'light in the darkness' are long gone.

But it is too easy to 'church bash': certainly, the experience of church can be poor for some, and there are those who have been hurt or damaged by it; but praise God for the many churches that are a credit to the Church's founder, churches which – however weakly – seek to serve their communities with grace and dignity.

2. Postmodern life

If you have attended any Christian conference in the last decade which attempted to help Christians take their faith seriously, then the subject of 'postmodernism' probably featured among the seminar topics. The word may seem academic or irrelevant, but there is no doubt that the reality of postmodernism has affected the Christian Church immensely in the last few decades. It is not my purpose to provide a lengthy analysis of the topic, even if I were able, but we do need to consider it broadly if we are to understand the climate in which every church is working in the UK today.

Postmodernism is a concept produced by diverse thinking in several different disciplines, and it is hard to define it in a way that captures its range of meaning. Postmodernism is especially concerned with truth: what we know, and how we know what we know. It is associated with thinkers such as Friedrich Nietzsche, Ludwig Wittgenstein, Jacques Derrida, Thomas Kuhn, Michel Foucault, Martin Heidegger and Jean-Francois Lyotard, and it is primarily a reinterpretation of what knowledge is and what counts as knowledge. Although some elements of 'postmodernist thinking' are matters of academic discussion in university philosophy departments, postmodern approaches to life affect British culture more than we perhaps realise.

To understand postmodernism today, we need to compare the way knowledge was understood in the past and how it is understood today. Philosophers have divided recent history into three phases: *pre-modern* (from the Middle Ages to the seventeenth and eighteenth centuries), *modern* (from the late seventeenth/early eighteenth centuries to the 1970s), and *postmodern* (from the 1970s into the future).

Up until the late seventeenth century, people in the Western world believed that there is a God who knows everything. They believed humans are finite beings who can know only a small part of what God knows. Our knowing was understood as a 'subset' of God's knowledge. Human knowledge was thought to come from what God reveals through the natural order, our reason, and the community in which we live.

Historians disagree about when modernity started, but do agree that there was a general shift in mindset, initiated by humankind's growing understanding of the physical universe, advances in science and agriculture, and ability to control the world. People started to question whether 'God' was a necessary part of our mental framework. Instead of starting with 'God', thinkers started with 'I'. The mantra of this era is 'I think therefore I am', a celebrated statement made by the French scientist and philosopher René Descartes (1596–1650). According to Descartes and other thinkers, scientific laws suggest that the physical world is a machine which the human mind can understand: such laws can be discovered and stated, helping us to describe our world and understand its processes. 'Truth' is both desirable and attainable: scientists can find things out, and this is good for humanity. This view assumes that truth about the world is 'universal' – the laws of physics apply in London, Paris and Washington, and as humans we are subject to them regardless of our culture, social standing or personal circumstances.

In the mid-nineteenth century some thinkers were suggesting that our increasing understanding of the natural world had removed the need for God. The work of Charles Darwin, in particular *Origin of the Species* (1859), his celebrated book which provided an alternative explanation for the creation of human beings to that of Genesis, seemed further evidence that we didn't need 'God' to explain, or reveal, truth. As scientific progress and Western scepticism about God continued, the twentieth century saw further erosion of the belief in a creator God. This, combined with critical studies of the Scriptures, undermined traditional belief in the supernatural.

Christians, for their part, countered these attacks on the credibility and authority of the Church. Some Christians responded by showing that Christianity is not anti-intellectual or anti-science. They believed that 'all truth is God's truth', so had no fear of investigating the natural world, seeing no conflict between the revelation of Scripture and the discoveries of good science. Some Christian scientists argued that the Bible's creation accounts do not specify the mechanisms used by God in creation, and theology can include elements of evolutionary thinking.

Historians give various dates for the rise of postmodernism: the roots of postmodern thought can be seen at various times within modernism. Some identify postmodern thinking as beginning in the 1930s, but most agree that it became especially prevalent during the 1970s, affecting many academic institutions in the next decades and slowly filtering into popular culture.

Postmodernism rejects the autonomous individualism of modernism, and all that follows from it. It doesn't see humanity as an ocean of individuals, but sees humans as 'social constructs'. By the postmodern account, we do not exist or think independently of the community with which we identify. In particular, postmodernism rejects 'meta-narratives' or overarching stories, such as those provided by the Bible, which suggest that truth is universal. Postmodernism suggests that truth is subjective: we all come to the Bible with different assumptions and understand it in different ways. Why should your reading of the Bible be imposed on me? Mine is different, but equally valid.

This is where postmodernism affects the culture we as Christians live in, and explains why so many people reject the Church. Once we question whether the Bible's revelation is authoritative, then the foundation of Christian belief is undermined. The Bible is seen as one of many sources of truth, and Christianity as just one of many pathways to truth. Indeed, postmodern philosophy would question whether the Bible has 'one meaning', because meaning depends on what we bring to the text, and what we read out of it. So ethical values based on Scripture are seen as not 'set in stone', but adjustable and adaptable according to different communities. This postmodern mindset is taught in schools and universities, and is a pervasive influence in contemporary films and music.

If you have been brought up in a postmodern world (and even if you haven't), you will think of the world as 'postmodern' without being aware that you are doing so – just as modernists used to unconsciously see the world in a largely scientific way.

Today, therefore, many people have an unconscious postmodern mindset: they see traditional evangelical churches, and church life in general, as incompatible with their view of the world. Christianity is based on an 'overarching meta-narrative' (a universal story) that Christians understand to be applicable to all people, everywhere, in every generation. This is certainly the view of most church leaders. Traditional Christianity teaches that the acceptance or rejection of the central message of our faith is the defining moment of a person's life, and urges people to focus exclusively on the Bible as the source of revelation for their lives, the standard of truth by which any other 'revelation' of 'truth' must be judged. Many church leaders would claim that their understanding of the Bible enables them to know, and tell other people, how we can best live our lives.

In these days when a 'politically correct' approach includes accepting all religions and lifestyles, the Church tells us that Jesus is the only Way to God, and the impression is given in some churches that those who deliberately reject faith in Jesus will face eternal punishment. In short, if someone has imbibed a postmodern view of the world, then the teaching and style of most churches will alienate them.

The extent to which churches are aware of the postmodern approach will vary, and many have welcomed some of the more positive elements of postmodernism. We will look later at a movement known as 'emerging church'. Doug Pagitt, pastor of Solomon's Porch Church in Minneapolis, USA, helpfully explains that 'emerging church' includes those who minister *to* postmoderns, *with* postmoderns, or *as* postmoderns.[2] So some churches positively embrace postmodern ideas, and welcome postmodern churchgoers who have been alienated by the traditional Church.

3. The effects of postmodernism

3.1 A RESISTANCE TO AUTHORITY AND INSTITUTIONS
One result of postmodernism is that behaviour patterns which used to be regarded as abhorrent have now, to some extent, been legitimised. Some resistance to authority has a godless dimension to it, but postmodern thinkers have claimed that modernist approaches to life have been unsuccessful. For example, the twentieth century saw more killing of humans by their fellow humans than during all previous centuries put

together. The old hierarchical, authoritarian forms of leadership were seen to fail, and the Church – itself hierarchical – failed just as other institutions did. Religious conflict throughout history and up to the present time shows that we should look to the future without the encumbrance of outmoded ways of thinking or believing – including Christianity.

So as a postmodern person you arrive at church, you are told to sit and watch and listen, and you will probably feel that this institution gives a high priority to authority, and a low priority to personal involvement. This is one reason why the highly successful Alpha course, with its discussion groups, has appealed more strongly to the postmodern mindset than traditional church services.

3.2 More individualism and greater pluralism

In his book *The Gagging of God*, D.A. Carson[3] explains in detail how postmodernism embraces a pluralistic outlook. If no text has the truth (because on a postmodern view no one text could have 'the whole truth'), then why put all your eggs in one theological basket? To continue the analogy, you are free to make your omelette with eggs from various chickens. Take a little Islam and a slice of Judaism, sprinkle a pinch of Hindusim, and lay the mixture on a bed of Christian values.

The postmodern mind does not see the philosophical contradictions of this approach.

The 'all religions lead to God' approach is a nonsense, given that the major world religions disagree about both the nature of God and what kind of 'road' leads to 'God'. We are certainly not respecting other people's faiths when we claim they all worship the same God. They patently do not.

But for many in the UK, who are aware that we are part of a 'global village', a pluralistic approach seems to be the only way ahead. Indeed, Prince Charles has strongly hinted that if he became king he would pledge to defend 'faiths' rather than 'the faith', because Britain contains such a wide variety of faiths and he would not want to alienate believers who are not Christian.

The pluralistic philosophy of postmodernism also encourages a 'do-it-yourself' spirituality; if you can take from other religions, you can also take from other philosophies: a little self-help, some New Age spirituality, a dab of 'positive thinking' from the latest book featured on your favourite TV chat show. You can construct your own way of living and your own faith rather as you put together your wardrobe of clothes, choosing from a range of outlets and constructing the person you want to be.

3.3 NEGATIVE MEDIA PORTRAYALS OF THE CHURCH

Do you want to join an organisation with a reputation for sexual abuse and bigoted attitudes to gays and lesbians? And it's demeaning towards women, apparently anti-science, and has committed terrible atrocities down the centuries. Put like that, you might be reluctant to sign up. But this is the image of the Church in many people's minds. If those people are ignorant of the excellent work the Church does on behalf of many needy people, then their view of it will be entirely negative. And their view is not deliberately skewed: this is just 'how they see it'.

Gabe Lyons suspected that non-Christians in the US were negative about Christianity, but he had no firm evidence. He told his friend David Kinnaman, a researcher with an evangelical organisation, that he was setting up a charity to find out how Christianity was seen. Would David lead the project? The book *UnChristian*[4] is the outcome, after three years of listening to what young adult Americans really think about Christianity. The book is not easy reading. Christians were seen as 'anti-homosexual' (the view of 91%), 'judgemental' (87%) and 'hypocritical' (85%). Lower-ranking comments included 'old fashioned', 'too involved in politics', 'out of touch with reality', 'insensitive to others', 'boring', 'not accepting of other faiths', and 'confusing'. There were positives: many found Christians 'friendly', and three-quarters agreed that Christians had 'good values'; but the image was overwhelmingly negative. Lyons' suspicion was confirmed: outsiders perceive Christianity as distinctly 'unChristian'– hence the book's title.

The research is thorough, drawn from twelve representative surveys of young adult (15 to 29) 'outsiders': atheists, people from other religions, and 'unchurched' adults – a group representing 24 million Americans. These perceptions were drawn from outsiders in a nation where Christianity is dominant (some 40% of Americans go to church each Sunday, compared to 10% in the UK), and where churches use radio and TV to communicate their message to the masses – which increases the potential for negative perceptions. It should be added that some concerns raised in the survey are unlikely to apply here – I doubt for example that Christians in the UK would be labelled 'too political'.

But the book gives compelling reasons why we in British churches should listen to outsiders. Kinnaman, the main author, acknowledges that we should be discerning about outsiders' perceptions, especially as their views may reflect a defensive response to the claims of Christ. But his insightful analysis is troubling, since most of the respondents had first-hand and repeated contact with Christians or churches. These are not comments of people ignorant of church life, or of churchgoers.

If a similar survey were conducted in the UK, would we come off any better? A generation ago, 'Christian' was synonymous with loving, caring, selfless and charitable – perhaps in some places in the UK it still is. But today words like arrogant, intolerant or bigoted would be used to describe a Christian. These research results remind us that when we talk to outsiders we need to be careful with terms like 'Christian' or 'evangelical', because for many people these words will not conjure up the warm, positive images that we would like. Even if you attend a church where people's sense of community is strong, and whose contribution to public life is positive, you may want to be discreet when someone enquires about your faith: 'I am a Christian' can evoke a wide range of images and assumptions, and you will need to explain yourself very carefully.

3.4 OUTSIDERS' PERCEPTIONS OF THE VALUE OF CHRISTIANITY

The postmodern philosophical outlook, combines with the Church's poor image, means few people believe that Christianity has much to say about life outside its narrow religious world. For your non-Christian friends, your attending church is 'nice for you' but of no more interest to them than if you played pool or joined a drama group. So it is 'countercultural' for church leaders to encourage members to consider their lifestyle and to involve God in all areas of their life: this goes against the grain of a society where faith has retreated from the public arena into the private sphere, and where individuals are encouraged to 'do their own thing'.

It is rare in our news culture for a church spokesperson to be asked to give an opinion on matters that are not perceived to be ecclesiastical. When it became apparent that the activities of banks had precipitated an economic crisis, church leaders were not asked to appear on, for example, BBC's *Newsnight* to discuss the moral aspects of the 'greed culture' which has been fostered in Western countries.

All this means that churchgoers who are wavering in their faith are not encouraged to feel good about what they believe: they might be tempted to leave the Church because it seems to be a minority interest, with a low status in society; and they might withdraw their support rather as they would switch their vote from a small and unsuccessful political party at a local election.

3.5 CHANGES IN THE USE OF SUNDAYS

Probably 99% of churches hold their major service on a Sunday. If you are a churchgoer, Sunday will be the day when you go to church. But the advent of Sunday opening hours for shops in the UK has meant that Sundays are like every other day of the week. Sport is played on a Sunday, including the nation's favourite spectator sport, football (though most matches are still played on a Saturday). My generation, growing up in the 1970s, typically played sport for our school during the week and on Saturdays, and rarely on a Sunday. Now, school matches have been replaced with teams run by parents: budding Wayne Rooneys play on Sundays when the pitches are free from the grown-ups.

The breakdown of marriage also plays a part in changing social habits. Sunday is the day when Dad sees the kids, or family members meet – sometimes having to travel considerable distances. So, whereas in a previous generation church attendance was one of the few activities that everyone did on a Sunday, church now competes with a multitude of other activities: from do-it-yourself to gardening, from sports events to visiting the children. Devout churchgoers may feel that a genuine 'church experience' surpasses any alternative, and that God can hold His own against any competing attraction; but many people who seldom or never come to church do not share our view.

4. Personal reasons

There are many personal reasons why someone leaves 'the Church', just as there are when people leave a particular church. Any one of the reasons listed earlier might be a tipping point which leads someone to say: 'That's it – I've finished with Church.' There may be a simple reason given: the church is judgmental, hypocritical, uncaring, middle-class – a 'catch-all' word to explain why this particular person has left the Church, and isn't coming back.

5. Spiritual reasons

Perhaps the saddest reason for people leaving the Church is that they no longer believe. We have noted already that an inadequate foundation to our faith is exposed when hard times come. When my wife and I lived in Bournemouth, our neighbours had no particular interest in church, but they once came with us to a Remembrance Service, the husband having served in the Second World War. It seemed strange that as a non-churchgoer he should attend this service with us: when we sat together in church he confided that he had lost his faith after seeing the awful horrors of war. He explained: 'I couldn't believe in God when I saw what He allowed.'

War, illness, tragedy and crisis will all test the faith of people. If faith is a fair-weather consolation, or wishful thinking that 'all will be well', then it is no surprise that faith falters when the storms of life come.

6. Ethnic and cultural changes

The apostle Paul was keen to persuade the Galatian believers that in Christ ethnic difference means nothing: 'You are all sons of God through faith in Christ Jesus, for all of you who were baptised into Christ have clothed yourselves with Christ. There is neither Jew nor Greek, slave nor free, male nor female, for you are all one in Christ Jesus. If you belong to Christ, then you are Abraham's seed, and heirs according to the promise' (Gal. 3:26–9).

Unfortunately, many churches struggle to put this ideal of integration into practice, and even if their hope is to integrate all races, members of minority groups may feel left out. If an ethnic minority group has a significant presence in a host nation, they tend to congregate with each other rather than with the indigenous population. In the UK, especially in Greater London, there are many black-majority churches where skin colour (rather than racial background) is a uniting factor, and there are Chinese, American, Polish or Korean churches, for example, where culture provides worshippers with additional common ground. It is sad that traditional churches have not been seen as more accommodating. If gathering to worship means reaching other worshippers with a similar background, then arguably churches for people of one ethnic group make sense. But if splits occur because of perceived prejudice, then there is a problem. Sadly, some people left the Church, having felt treated like second-class 'citizens of heaven' because of their race, colour or class; and some of these leavers felt so deeply wounded that they didn't come back to the Church.

7. Political and legal influences

It is unusual for someone to leave a church in the UK because of a political stance taken by the church leadership. But it is possible, and since it happens in other parts of the world it is worth considering. In the United States there is a division between Republicans and Democrats on the issue of abortion, with Republicans typically more supportive of anti-abortion legislation than Democrats. Many American evangelicals have seen this as a key issue when deciding who to vote for. In some parts of the world, supporting one particular party is almost part of the Church's 'unwritten constitution'. For Protestants in Northern Ireland, supporting the Ulster Unionists or the Democratic Unionists was seen as mandatory, at a time when religious sectarianism divided communities. Even if partisan politics are not such an issue in other parts of the UK, a churchgoer may nonetheless feel that their strongly held political opinion is not shared by the majority in their church: and this can be sufficiently alienating for them to leave it.

8. Demographic changes: age

We have considered already how young people leave the Church because it seems alien to their subculture. Equally, older people may leave the Church because their own church has changed. Some prefer the service as it used to be; others dislike changes in musical style, or even an increase in volume. Changes in the layout and furniture of the church can be alienating: it was said of older people, at a time when rows of seats were replaced by chairs, that 'they left the church when the pews did'. For many older folk facing incremental change, living in a world they no longer recognise, the church is their one place of security: they prefer to worship as they always have done, and find it difficult to 'connect with God' through newer forms of worship.

Questions for discussion

1. Which of the social and cultural factors discussed in this chapter do you think affect your church?
2. How aware is your church, and the leaders in particular, of these issues?
3. Why has the Church been so slow to respond to major spiritual and cultural changes over the last forty years?
4. Are you resigned to a losing battle, or do you feel that your church can survive wider social changes?

SOME VISIONS OF THE FUTURE

This book has considered the reasons for people leaving local churches, and presents possible solutions for churches and church leaders. In this chapter we focus on the responses churches are making to the 'back-door' problem.

Having been active in ten churches, and served in pastoral ministry in three, I know how resistant a church can be to change of any kind. You can't blame church leaders who say they prefer things to remain as they are – 'anything for a quiet life!' However, declining numbers give a church the chance to examine its structure and focus; even if your numbers are constant at the moment, you might consider whether some of the influences outlined in this book might lead to decline in the future.

To bring change, we need a vision. Dieticians suggest displaying a picture of a slim person on the fridge door to help you resist the temptation of Ben and Jerry's ice cream. The popularity of do-it-yourself and house makeover programmes shows how we are inspired to copy in our own homes what we see on TV. So in this chapter I hope to show how some churches have responded to the forces in culture and society that cause people to leave their own church, or the Church. I will leave God to ignite your imagination to inspire change in *your* church.

Churches can follow one of three broad routes into the future:

- **Route One:**   Look back to go forward
- **Route Two:**   Recognise present realities
- **Route Three:**   Equip for future change

Route One: Look back to go forward

Many churches believe it is important to follow the pathways they have always trodden, and there are good reasons for this. Many of these pathways embody truths which the historic Church has forged through the centuries. Such churches are comfortable being who they are, within their traditional denomination or as part of the 'New Church stream'.

In some cases the trend of looking back has become more pronounced, with some evangelical/charismatic churches returning to the 'ancient paths' of pre-Reformation Christianity, before the 1500s. While stopping short of joining the Catholic Church, they have recognised that some of the writings and practices of pre-Reformation saints have much to teach us, and they are happy to accept them when they are backed by Scripture. Some churchgoers, especially those in the 'emerging Church',[1] are learning to value the art and symbolism associated with Catholic and High Church settings. Others see value in the ancient practices of fasting, meditation, solitude and silence as ways of developing their walk with God. In *Punk Monk: New Monasticism and the Ancient Art of Breathing*,[2] Andy Freeman and Pete Greig chart the rise of 'Boiler Rooms' – worship locations where prayer is continual and a community is built on disciplines of prayer, study, celebration and caring for the poor and lost – a pattern remarkably similar to that of an ancient monastery. From a humble beginning in Reading, southern England, there are now fifty-six Boiler Rooms in fourteen countries. Pete Greig was the pioneer of the '24/7 prayer movement', now a staple of many worship groups throughout the world.

There are some signs of unity between evangelical/charismatic churches and High Church/Catholic churches. On 8 February 1952, C.S. Lewis wrote to the *Church Times* of the great unity that existed between the 'High' (Anglo-Catholic) and 'Low' (evangelical) Churches, over against the 'liberal' and 'anti-supernatural' churches. He used the phrases 'Deep Church' or 'Mere Christianity' to describe their common faith. Recently, the term Deep Church has been revived to describe the truths shared by a range of Church traditions, such as Catholic, Protestant and Orthodox. It seems that in our times there is a return to this unity.

Some postmodern Christians are seeing the value of symbolism and art in worship, which help to engage all the senses in worshipping God. But many churches are sticking to the ancient paths because they fear that postmodernity represents at best a cul de sac, and at worst a cliff edge, for the Christian Church. In general, church people reinstating previous traditions can be divided into (i) those who preserve both theology and practice, and (ii) those who preserve the theology but are eclectic about its expression in worship.

Ron tells the story of the Salvation Army group in Sydney who insisted on open-air preaching with a band accompaniment, although no one was listening. This seems perverse.

Rather than asking 'How does Jesus want us to fulfil the Great Commission today?', some prefer to operate as they always have done – which worked at one time, but may need serious modification today. Billy

Graham, responding to criticism of his evangelism, said: 'I prefer the way I do it to the way you don't do it!' This should restrain us from being critical of believers who use strategies we don't – for example, those who have the courage to share the gospel in the open air. When it is clear that people are not listening to us, we need to find more effective means of communication – and learn from other churches.

The preservation of former methods includes the service style. Whereas a poor *evangelistic* strategy is obvious because new people don't come, it is less obvious when the style of *worship* isn't working, because we have a captive audience. We assume that if worship practices are 'biblical' (depending on how this is defined), then they should be maintained. With this logic, if people do leave, then it must be 'their fault' for not following 'God's way' – including what is sung, who leads the service, who preaches, how long the sermon is, and every other element of the service. I have heard traditional practices defended on scriptural grounds: 'if it was good enough for the apostle Paul, then it's good enough for me' – even when the practice in question originated in the twentieth century! At other times I have heard people dismiss a worship style with the comment 'we prefer not to do it like that', as if the church is a gentleman's club whose members must wear a tie and only smoke in certain rooms. This rule-bound approach would steer a church steadily into the future, oblivious to the world around. Its members would be encouraged (forced, even) to continue with archaic and irrelevant practices, confident that if they are 'true to Scripture' then God will accept them.

Route Two: Recognise present realities

A second category of churches pay a lot of attention to the present scene. They assess the state of congregational life in the light of the church's perceived mission, and ask: 'How are we doing?' As numbers decline, and the average age of churchgoers increases, they ask: 'What do we need to do to reach the average person, who has grown up with little knowledge of the Bible, and has minimal awareness of life's deeper meanings?' Such churches are not open to changing what they *believe* – they are still happy Anglicans or Baptists or Methodists or Pentecostals; but they are looking to change the way they *operate*.

In the latter part of the twentieth century a number of movements have affected the Church in the UK and the West. These are worth considering because of their impact on churches today.

UP A CREEK

In 1991 I visited South Barrington, in the northwest suburbs of Chicago, to see a church which had grown from 100 young people in 1975 into a 'mega-church' of over 10,000. Today, about 18,000 worshippers attend weekend services, and many more watch a video of the sermon on five additional campuses in the Chicago area. Founded and led by Bill Hybels, Willow Creek Community Church had as their centrepiece a 'seeker service' every Sunday, designed to reach those seeking God – people who were unfamiliar with Christian language, and could not sing songs expressing beliefs they had not yet embraced. The worship services for believers took place midweek, so the focus of the church's activities was on 'the unchurched'. In 1992 I joined hundreds of other believers at the NEC, Birmingham, for the first UK-based Willow Creek Conference. After that conference, some UK churches started applying the principles that underpinned the Willow Creek approach.

Willow Creek forced churches to ask whether their style of church was appropriate for those outside the faith, framed in the challenging question: 'Would your members invite their non-Christian friends to a service here?'

The Willow Creek model trained church members to build relationships with non-believers, using verbal testimonies of their faith to invite 'seekers' to a service designed for them. The service had minimal congregational singing – perhaps one song at the start, whose lyrics would not alienate outsiders – and the content might include drama and/or video clips, focusing on an area of life likely to be interesting to a seeker; the songs would identify with the theme of the service; the talk would start where seekers are, aiming to build empathy with them before outlining what the Bible has to say: sometimes providing an opportunity to trust Christ for the first time, but not always. Willow Creek calculated that on average it took a non believer six months of attending weekly services to reach the point where they were able to make a decision for Christ.

Following this model, many UK churches have adjusted their activities to become more deliberately focused on those outside the Church. From 1995 to 1996 I served as associate pastor at Waterfront Church, Southampton, which embraced the seeker-centred model and operated for four years as the first church of this kind in the UK, with occasional support from Willow Creek staff. Though few UK churches followed the approach so fully, many were changed by it. Bill Hybels says he wants churches to apply the principles, working them out in their own setting. In fact my church in Southampton became exhausted with the weekly seeker-targeted model and changed its approach considerably – but it still retained an outward-looking focus. Two organisations were spawned through Willow Creek's influence: the Willow Creek Association UK and Ireland (WCUK) organises regular conferences, and provides resources for churches and individuals; and the annual Willow Creek Leadership Summit is shown via DVD in venues across the UK and Ireland. There are nearly 900 churches listed in the WCUK. Reaching the Unchurched Network (RUN) has no formal links with Willow Creek, though it has good relations with WCUK and typically uses UK-based leaders to run conferences and provide resources for churches.

THE FUTURE'S ORANGE?

Another US church that has made its mark in the UK is Saddleback Community Church in Orange County, south of Los Angeles. In 1980 Rick Warren and his wife arrived to plan a church for the new estates being built in the county. Starting with home-based Bible study, the church soon took off, and by the time he was ready to write his book, *Purpose Driven Church* (1995), there were well over 10,000 members. Many will know Rick Warren through his second book, *Purpose Driven Life*,[3] which has sold 30 million copies. The basic premise of the 'Purpose Driven' paradigm is that the Church needs to recognise God's purposes emerging through key characteristics in the lives of people in its care. Two commands drive the approach: the 'Great Commandment' (Matthew 22:39 – 'Love your neighbour as yourself') and the 'Great Commission' (Matthew 28:19 – 'make disciples of all nations'). Armed with these commands, Warren sees five main purposes for the Church today: worship, ministry, mission, fellowship and discipleship. Today, the church he still serves is an evangelical congregation averaging 22,000 weekly attendees, with a

120-acre campus and more than 300 community ministries to groups such as prisoners, business leaders, addicts, single parents, and HIV/AIDS sufferers. Having sought an evangelical minister to pray at his inauguration the new president of the USA, Barack Obama, chose Rick Warren.

The Saddleback style of service has some similarities to Willow Creek's, and when I attended with my wife in 2001 the mix of songs, video, drama and talk were reminiscent of what I had experienced at Willow Creek, though songs were much more worship-focused. What is distinctive is their strategy of taking a seeker through faith to maturity stage by stage via a series of classes, helping the new believer to realise who they are in Christ, how they can grow, and how they can serve God.

The UK response to the 'Purpose Driven' ethos has not been as strong as with Willow Creek, but many churches find the approach amenable because it involves a less radical restructuring of services, and focuses on areas where most Christians are in agreement: worship, ministry, mission, fellowship and discipleship. Many churches have appreciated the deliberate balance which is encouraged between these aspects of Christianity; Warren argues that we need to give appropriate time and resources to any given area – so that, for example, mission is not missed out, but neither is it the top priority. Even churches not wanting radical restructuring have benefited from the Purpose Driven Church UK partnership, which offers courses involving just over six weeks of focused activity and teaching. Hundreds of UK churches have followed the programmes 'forty days of purpose', 'forty days of community', or 'forty days of love' – all concepts created and outlined by Rick Warren.

A CELL-OUT?

A 'cell church' is based on the regular meetings of cell groups, typically of ten to fifteen Christians. This is distinct from churches who use the words 'cell group' to describe their home groups: rather, it is a way of organising a whole church into small groups which have specific beliefs and functions, led by people equipped for the task.

There are many branches of the 'cell-church' movement, one of the best known – because of its perceived success in the 'G12 movement' – being based in Bogota, Colombia. Cesar Castellanos developed the 'G12 strategy' after visiting the Yoido Full Gospel Church led by David Yonggi

Cho, who used a cell-church structure for his huge mega-church in South Korea. Castellanos returned to his church, the Mission Carismatica Internacional in Bogota, and implemented a strategy he believed God had given him. From 1991 to 1994 his church grew from 70 to 1,200 members and by 1999 it had 20,000 cells, with a regular weekly church congregation of 45,000 people.

The rationale is that the main leader would disciple 12 people in Christian values, teachings, prayer and ministry on a weekly basis until each was ready to lead their own group. Each disciple would find 12 new disciples and repeat the same process until there were 144, and so on. In both theory and practice, this process enabled the church to grow exponentially.

The G-12 movement itself has been controversial, but many other churches have embraced the idea that smaller units of fellowship which aim to support one another can be effective in evangelism, in a way that larger church groups are not. Indeed as we have seen, the Early Church groups were probably similar in size, meeting as they did in believers' houses. In 1995 the first British National Cell Conference took place in Harpenden, Hertfordshire, attended by 250 leaders from a variety of churches. This gave birth to Cell UK, an organisation to serve the cell-church movement. Originally a department of Youth with a Mission, Cell UK is now an independent organisation and charity. Perhaps the best-known church to embrace cell-church principles is Kensington Temple, an Elim Pentecostal church in west London. According to its website:[4]

In September 2003, Kensington Temple, London City Church completed a three-year transition into the G12 model of cell church, having grown to 11,000 people in 1,800 cells. With around 70% of the church active in cells the leadership were well on their way to achieve their goal of maximum mobilization. Since then, the main thrust of the life and ministry of the church is through the cells. These cells are considered tiny units of 'church' doing everything that 'church' should be doing. Cells are now where the evangelism, discipleship, pastoral care and prayer life of the Kensington Temple takes place.

RENEWAL

If the Willow Creek, 'Purpose Driven' and cell models are examples of changes in church structure and approach, it is also clear that many fellowships have been reborn through a changed expectation of God's work.

For many Christians, self-evaluation led to the discovery that God was at work in key churches, and their leaders, in ways they had not imagined. We don't have space here to chart the rise of the charismatic movement in the UK from the 1960s to the present day,[5] and it is unwise to generalise about a movement that has many facets to it. In some cases the 'house churches' (also called 'New Churches' – though some are fifty years old!) effected a total theological makeover, convincing believers that God was restoring to the Church the ethos seen in Acts, and commissioning apostles and prophets to oversee the expansion of God's kingdom. More recent approaches have been less triumphalistic and less insulated from the mainstream denominations, many of whom have embraced the more recent theology – with a greater expectation of tongues, prophecy and healing in churches today.

Many principles of the 'New Church' movement have been accepted by churches in mainstream denominations. Since the first wave of change in the 1960s and 1970s, other theological currents have reached UK shores.

VINEYARD SPREADS

In the 1980s John Wimber arrived in the UK from the US, and caused a stir by teaching that 'signs and wonders' should be part of the Church's lifestyle. Wimber, a former Calvary Chapel Church pastor, had been challenged to expect the miraculous gifts of the Bible to be evident today, and following some ten months' praying for the sick when nothing happened, he saw a breakthrough leading to regular healings and other miracles in his church in California. Many Christians in the UK were inspired by this approach, some adopting greater supernatural expectation into their existing church structures – including many Anglican churches which now form the unofficial network of New Wine – while others formally joined the Vineyard Movement of Churches which Wimber helped to found. This comprises 1,500 Vineyard churches worldwide, with 600 in the US and about 90 in the UK.

CANADA CHARISMA

In January 1994 there were reports that a church of 300 at the end of a runway at Pearson International Airport in Toronto had been 'visited by God'. Though descriptions of what happened are still disputed, the effects have been astonishing. Known as the 'Toronto Blessing' and described as a 'transferrable anointing', it overcame worshippers with outbreaks of laughter, weeping, groaning, shaking, falling, and what seemed like 'drunkenness'.

The 'renewal' came to what was the Toronto Airport Vineyard (now The Toronto Airport Christian Fellowship) when a visiting US pastor, Randy Clark of St Louis, Missouri, came for what was planned as a series of four meetings. It led to a marathon series of services held every night of the week except Monday from January until March, when Clark had to return to St Louis. Critics latched on to the fact that worshippers were making animal noises, notably barking, though Clark claims this happened only a handful of times, and was a distraction from what he believes God was doing in those services.[6]

In early September of 1995, cumulative attendance reached about 600,000, including approximately 20,000 Christian leaders and 200,000 first-time visitors from virtually every country and denomination. Within twenty months of the beginning of this outpouring of the Holy Spirit, 9,000 people had made a first-time commitment to Christ at the Toronto Airport Vineyard. Church membership tripled in size to about 1,000 regular members, from 360 in early 1994.

The effects of the Toronto Blessing quickly became international in scope. Within a year of the 'outpouring', an estimated 4,000 churches representing all main denominations in the UK were touched by the renewal, and many today are part of the 'Toronto Network'. The Toronto Blessing has spread not only to Britain but to many other countries. The international arm of Toronto Airport Christian Fellowship, known as Catch The Fire Ministries, has affiliates in the UK including a new church in Wembley, London.

This brief snapshot of specific movements reminds us that for some, changing church styles and structures have dovetailed with a changing view and expectation of a God who refreshes and restores the Church to be a powerful body to serve in the world. Weekly services are seen to 'give room' for the Holy Spirit to work, and worshippers in these new churches believe that the divine power manifested through prayer, prophecy, words of knowledge and miraculous healing equips the Church to do God's purposes, and reveals the reality of God to those who were far from Him. These new church initiatives have not always been embraced by the evangelical community in the UK, but no one can deny their impact.

Route Three: Equip for future change

Does the Church in the West need a radical solution? That depends on the size of the problem the Church faces.

For many, there is an awareness that the Church as it exists is not working, both because it is out of place in today's cultural landscape, and because its traditional approaches, whatever their biblical merit, leave out key elements. But many church leaders have woken up to the realities of contemporary culture, and are inspired by what they see God doing in their own churches; they would say their more flexible approach equips them for the future. So Willow Creek and Saddleback, for example, will adjust their style according to the changing needs of their church family and the wider community. Both churches have more recently begun to be especially concerned to help the poor and disadvantaged. Churches affected by and embracing renewal will confidently expect God to continue touching people in the future, as He does now and always has done. They would argue that their job is to remain 'hungry for God', and open to His direction.

But there is a stream of thought that a more radical view of 'church' is required if we are to win the present postmodern generation.

Emerging church

Before writing their book *Emerging Churches: Creating Community in Postmodern Cultures*,[7] Eddie Gibbs and Ryan K. Bolger spent five years researching what are loosely known as 'emerging churches', ie gatherings of Christians who are trying to live out their faith in ways they believe are appropriate in a postmodern culture. The book includes some fifty communities from both sides of the Atlantic, though it is hard to quantify them, and the authors admit that some leaders they interviewed are reluctant to have their churches described as 'emerging'. The term encompasses a broad group of beliefs and activities, and overlaps with such descriptions as 'new ways of being church', 'fresh expressions of church', and 'future church'. We have noted already how Doug Pagitt, pastor at Solomon's Porch in Minneapolis, helpfully explains that the 'emerging church' includes those who minister *to* postmoderns, *with* postmoderns, and *as* postmoderns.

The vast majority of 'emerging churches' fit the first two of Pagitt's categories. They are orthodox in their views of Jesus and the Bible. It is typically the third group that attracts criticism: church leaders who have chosen to minister *as* postmoderns, embracing the idea that we cannot know absolute truth, or that we cannot know truth absolutely, and emphasising that our own experience determines what we bring to, and how we read, any text – including Scripture. This notion of subjective understanding is what raises concerns.

The 'emerging church' wants to redefine church theology, worship and activities. Some such churches have a more 'High Church' approach, with candles and incense, sacred space, and the use of imagery and sacred objects. Other churches give priority to how a person lives rather than what they say they believe, quoting passages like Matthew 25:45 where Jesus speaks of helping 'the least of these': caring for those in need is more important than quoting Bible verses, or stating credal beliefs. 'By their fruits [not their theology] you will know them.' So leaders of 'emerging churches' ask: 'Is evangelicalism really creating disciples like the ones Jesus described?'

Gibbs and Bolger list the following nine core practices as features of the 'emerging churches' they observed:

1   Identifying with Jesus (and His way of life)
2   Transforming secular space (overcoming the secular/sacred split)
3   Living as community (not 'strangers in proximity' at a church service)
4   Welcoming the stranger (radical, gentle and inclusive hospitality)
5   Serving with generosity (not serving the institution called 'church', but people)
6   Participating as producers (not 'widgets' in the church system)
7   Creating as created beings
8   Leading as a body (beyond the hierarchical or 'controlling' model of leadership)
9   Merging ancient and contemporary spiritualities

To quote Gibbs and Bolger: 'Emerging churches destroy the Christendom idea that church is a place, a meeting or a time. Church is a way of life, a rhythm, a community, a movement.'[8]

Gibbs and Bolger outline the way 'modernity' began by creating the idea of secular space, that is, space where God does not reign or is not welcomed. This idea marginalised the Church, driving it into a private arena, and this separation led to the 'sacred/secular' divide.

It would be hard to examine 'future church' without mentioning the work of Tom Sine. In his book *The New Conspirators* (IVP 2008)[9] Sine lists four streams: Monastic, Mosaic, Missional Church, and Emerging Church. He argues that the defining reality found in each of these movements, is the move away from an inward or attractional 'come-to-us' approach. Instead, all these streams have recovered an understanding of mission that recognizes the cosmic proportion of Christ's life, death and resurrection. This has enabled many younger Christians to switch from a 'me first' focus on personal achievement and advancement to discerning the activity of God in the world, and joining God in that activity to bring about global healing and wholeness.

Exponents of 'emerging churches' are clear that something radical needs to be done if the Church – however defined – is to survive and prosper in our postmodern Western world. No one really knows the size of the 'emerging churches' movement, but many who have left traditional churches have found a home there, and these churches are here to stay.

FRESH EXPRESSIONS

The Church of England's response to declining numbers in the UK was to launch 'Fresh Expressions' in conjunction with the Methodist Church, whose loss of members was even greater. This initiative was launched in 2004 as both an acknowledgement of and response to changing patterns of community, culture and worship: in particular, the recognition that traditional Sunday morning worship was no longer the norm for many people. 'Fresh Expressions' sought to provide a church experience for people in diverse places, and in the kind of networks that more typically reflect today's society. This diversity was reflected in a new range of worship options: located in schools or cafés, focusing on young people or alternative worship styles, and offering midweek or weekend services.

'Fresh Expressions' involves features such as:

- The renewal of an existing congregation through mission, and especially through careful listening to the non-churchgoers the congregation is called to serve. This might involve radically reshaping the provision of all-age worship, for instance, or rethinking a midweek service.
- Reinventing an existing 'fringe' group, mission project or community service so that it is no longer a stepping-stone to Sunday church, but becomes 'church' in its own right.
- A youth group might grow into a youth congregation, or a lunch club for the elderly might provide worship after the meal.
- Creating a new Christian community within a single parish or circuit, as a mission initiative. Often it will be lay-led and have a relatively small budget.
- An informal service in a local leisure centre and a midweek after-school meeting for a meal and worship would be two examples of new styles of worship.
- A large mission initiative spanning several parishes or circuits will probably require a full-time paid post and a substantial budget.
- There could be a new network church across a city centre for Generation X, a town-wide teenage congregation, or a home-based church planted on a new housing estate.

The 'Fresh Expresions' website lists three examples of fresh expressions:[10]

- An Alpha course was held in a teashop in a former mining town in Nottinghamshire. Several years and several Alpha courses on, a new church continues to meet in the teashop on a weekday evening, its members now leading and supporting successive Alpha courses.
- A Church of England minister wanted to build 'church' without a building. With his bishop's blessing he now leads a network church centred round students and young professionals in Bristol. Meeting in a coffee house is just one way in which this new church is made accessible to newcomers.
- A central Birmingham network church meets in bars and cafés. It draws on members' personal contacts to create a community where all are

welcome, whatever their stage of faith. Accepting the transitional nature of city life, this church seeks to accompany growing Christians.

There is clearly some overlap between 'Fresh Expressions' and 'emerging church'. The former describe the latter in these terms:

- Those who think and write about Christianity and our changing culture; they are wrestling with the challenges presented to the Christian faith by postmodern thought and behaviour. How can the gospel connect with today's world? What might be the implications for church?
- Those exploring new forms of church mainly with people who still go to church (but who are often about to leave); typically they are into alternative forms of worship and authentic community. Many have a heart for mission, but their starting point is to work with Christians who are dissatisfied with existing church.
- Those exploring new forms of church mainly for or with people who don't attend church; some of these innovative forms of church have a fruitful track record, but others are small, young and fragile. Though not everyone would use the term, we would describe these communities as 'fresh expressions of church'.

CHURCH RE-SHAPED

In *The Shaping of Things to Come: Innovation and Mission for the Twenty-first-century Church* (2003)[11] Michael Frost and Alan Hirsch also take a radical look at contemporary church life, arguing that merely tinkering with the modern Church is never going to provide a Church that is adequate for today's Western world. They argue that it is revolution, not evolution, that is required – quoting Einstein that 'the kind of thinking that will solve the world's problems will be of a different order than the kind that created those problems in the first place'.

Their starting point is an understanding of God: 'Our Christology determines our missiology and our missiology our ecclesiology.' They see God as a 'sending being' – sending His Son to earth to be incarnate in our world, and then sending His people out in mission with the message about Himself. 'Mission is not merely an activity of the church, it is the very heartbeat and work of God ... God is a sending God, with a desire to see humankind and creation reconciled, redeemed and healed.'

In typical churches today we operate on a 'come to us' model: 'We have the truth, come and hear it: we have the presence of God, come and enjoy it.' Not so much 'reaching out' as 'dragging in'! As well as being merely 'attractional', the church has become dualistic: operating as if life can be divided into the spiritual or sacred, and the secular, rather than seeing Jesus as Lord of all. As a result Christians lead compartmentalised lives, presuming that God is present in church but not in the office, that clergy are God's full-time workers, but accountants aren't, that Sunday is a day of worship, but Monday isn't.

Frost and Hirsch also question the heavily hierarchical structures of modern church life – a classic feature of Anglican organisation but also, they argue, pervasive in many other denominations and even in 'New Church' streams.

If we agree that new paradigms are needed for church today, Frost and Hirsch describe some fascinating ways in which Christians take mission seriously. They claim that church needs to be *incarnational, messianic* and *apostolic*:

1. The 'missional' church is *incarnational*, not 'attractional', in its ecclesiology. It does not create sanctified spaces into which believers must come to encounter the gospel. Rather, the missional church disassembles itself and seeps into the cracks and crevices of a society in order to be Christ to those who don't yet know him.

2. The missional church is *messianic*, not dualistic, in its spirituality. That is, it adopts the world-view of Jesus the Messiah, rather than that of the Greco-Roman empire. Instead of seeing the world as divided between the sacred (religious) and profane (non-religious), like Christ it sees the world and God's place in it as holistic and integrated.

3. The missional church adopts an *apostolic*, rather than hierarchical, mode of leadership. By 'apostolic' is meant a mode of leadership that recognizes the fivefold gifts detailed by Paul in Ephesians 4. It abandons the triangular hierarchies of the traditional church and embraces a biblical, 'flat-leadership' community that unleashes the gifts of evangelism, apostleship and prophecy, as

well as the pastoral and teaching gifts that are currently popular. In contrast to the cultural imperialism of many past missional efforts, the authors advocate a 'radical rethink about the symbols, language, metaphors, vernacular and idioms we employ when presenting Christ to our world':

So much reflection on Jesus portrays a man who is overly serious, who wrung his hands a lot ... rather, his was a very attractive spirituality ... He was notorious for hanging out with the wrong types ... We need his model of holy laughter, ... his sheer love of life, ... his infectious holiness, ... his common people's religion ... We partner with God in the redemption of the world.'[12]

It would be a radical step for churches to start at the very beginning and examine what their churches actually are – are they, to use Frost and Hirsch's term, 'missional communities', or merely companies of people who unthinkingly affirm the same doctrines, listen to the same sermons, sing the same songs and carry out the same tasks? If we sought a new orientation, we would be different from many, or even most, churches in the UK.

THINKING THROUGH WHAT WE SAY

Sooner or later, discussions about mission in the twenty-first century touch on the subject of 'contextualisation'. Frost and Hirsch define it thus:

Contextualisation can be defined as the dynamic process whereby the constant message of the gospel interacts with specific relative human situations. It involves an examination of the gospel in the light of the respondent's world-view and then adapting the message, encoding it in such a way that it can become meaningful to the respondent.[13]

Rene Padilla, in *Mission Between the Times* puts it this way: 'Contextualisation is when the gospel presented, and the response called for, offends for the right reasons and not the wrong ones'.[14]

To bring these definitions down to earth: you might think that telling someone that Jesus died for their sins is part of a faithful telling of the gospel.

But if someone thinks that Jesus is the name of a Spanish footballer, and has no concept of sin, their world-view makes it impossible for them to understand that message. You would need to explain who Jesus is, what sin is, and why His death has something to do with them. If you told a non-believer that to hear about Jesus they must wear a suit and attend a special building to listen to a man in a dress, called a cassock, they are unlikely to accept your offer: the way the gospel is typically presented is alien to an inner-city youth who has no suit, and would find a man dressed in a frock bizarre!

American 'emerging church' leaders Brian McLaren and Leonard Sweet focus on the issue of contextualisation: they see it as necessary for any overseas mission enterprise, and also as needing to be done in the UK and other Western contexts. We may speak the same language as those around us, but the grid through which they hear us is so shaped by the postmodern non-church mindset that others cannot understand what we are saying, or will misinterpret it.

MEGA-CHURCH

A mega-church is a church typically defined as having about 2,000 or more attendees for a typical weekly service. There are at least twenty such churches in the UK, including Kingsway International Christian Centre in east London, and Kensington Temple and Holy Trinity Brompton (the base for Alpha), both in west London. Hartford Institute's database lists more than 1,300 such Protestant churches in the United States. Some observers argue that one feature of the future Church in the UK is increasingly large churches. Christian Research found that increasing numbers of believers are attending larger churches. Congregations of more than 400 account for only 4% of churches in the UK, but proportionately 25% of the church-going population.[15] The reasons are not hard to find: in a consumerist culture we will shop for the church that meets our needs, and the mega-churches are the Tesco of our day, offering a wide range of options for all the family.

Larger churches have many advantages: staff resources to meet the needs of various sectors of the church; an abundance of volunteers enabling members to serve where they prefer, and not where there's a gap to fill; vibrant worship, with a full range of musical and multimedia input; and the opportunity to meet people of one's own age: parents can rest assured that their children/teenagers are not left to struggle in a multi-age 'junior church' group. And with all these opportunities, you can if you want remain gloriously anonymous and disengaged from church life.

For many, the large size of the church provides a visible reminder that their faith in God is not strange, but shared by many others; and it can be (though isn't necessarily) an easy place to invite interested friends. However, critics of these large churches raise challenging questions:

- It is easy to get lost in a big church: are they truly 'churches' in the New Testament sense if it is possible to be so anonymous that you are never called to work out your faith with other worshippers?
- Can the leaders truly be 'shepherds of God's flock' when perhaps they only know the names of a minority of members?
- Doesn't the leadership resemble the board of a company, rather than a team of godly servants?
- Don't large churches suck the life out of smaller churches nearby, who lose members because they are unable to meet their needs on the same scale?

Against these objections, it could be argued that large churches have become large because they are healthy. As Rick Warren reminds us in *Purpose Driven Church*, if a living thing is healthy, it will grow. Of course there are churches that increase their membership because of members transferring from other churches, but in general people attend big churches – and stay – because they are being fed and nurtured, and the church grows because it is able to win people to Christ, and nurture those who come to faith in Him.

Post-congregational Church?

It may seem odd to consider people who have left the Church – after all we are looking to 'close the back door', not reflecting on those who have already left. But when we envisage the Church of the future it seems likely that one trend will continue: many Christians will practise their faith without regular contact and interaction with other Christians in a congregational setting. George Barna suggests that some 5% of US believers are in this category, and anecdotal evidence suggests there is a sizeable minority of 'post-congregational' Christians in the UK too. Worldwide, author-researcher David Barrett estimates that 112 million people are 'churchless Christians'. That could be 5% worldwide, a proportion which might double by 2025 if current trends continue.[16]

There is a groundswell of change that is radically altering the Christian landscape. Parts of the Church are moving from an institutional, congregational model as practised for centuries, towards simpler structures which evoke a much earlier form of Christianity. In George Barna's words:

> *The local church has virtually no discernible influence on people's lives ... One million people leave the traditional church each year ... These Christians reject historical denominationalism and all restrictive central authority, and attempt to lead a life of following Jesus, seeking a more effective missionary lifestyle. They are the fastest-growing Christian movements in the world.*[17]

Barna identifies seven main influences on our thoughts and actions in contemporary culture: movies, television, music, family, books, law, and the Internet. Barna's research indicates that the local church has virtually no influence on people's lives. Consequently, the Church is competing with strong forces in trying to facilitate spiritual transformation in people's lives.

GONE FOR GOOD?
Churchless Faith, by Alan Jamieson,[18] is a book that brings research findings to bear on this issue. The research was conducted for Jamieson's doctoral thesis, and focuses on people who have left what the author calls 'EPC' (evangelical, Pentecostal and charismatic) churches. He groups these types of churches together based on their similarities, and because they are the growing sectors of Christianity worldwide. The data for the book comes from interviews with 108 church leavers and 54 church leaders in Jamieson's home country of New Zealand.

Interestingly, many of the church leavers had held positions of leadership in the church. They had been involved at the heart of church life – as pastors, pastors' wives or missionaries – and had spent on average sixteen years in the church. Of these, 70% were aged between 35 and 45 years, 94% had been church leaders, and 40% had spent one year or more as a full-time (paid) Christian worker for a local church, para-church group or overseas missionary organization, or had studied full-time in a theological institution. Many had been both theologial students and church leaders.

Jamieson discovered that most of the leavers had definitely not 'lost their faith'. Most would pray regularly, read the Bible, and even engage in 'Christian' activities outside church life. They saw faith as a pilgrimage, but believed that 'church' did not help them at this stage of their journey.

He groups the leavers into four categories: 'disillusioned followers', 'reflective exiles', 'transitional explorers' and 'integrated wayfinders'. 'Disillusioned followers' listen to Christian music, watch Christian TV, go to seminars and relate to other Christians, but do not go to church services or take part in 'Christian activities' – or if they do, do so privately. Jamieson describes this group as having an 'unexamined faith', and being 'very bold' both before they had left church and afterwards. They go to inter-denominational events, move on quickly, and are never satisfied. They rate their prophetic gifts highly, readily telling church leaders where they are wrong!

'Reflective exiles' are a group who are 'deconstructing their faith'. They are questioning and tentative about issues of faith. Unlike 'disillusioned followers' they repudiate the faith they had espoused as members of an 'EPC' church, and they now reject anything that reminds them of those days.

'Transitional explorers' are 'inner-dependent'. They don't know what or who they can trust outside themselves, but they trust their own faith or intellect. They are called 'explorers' because of their tendency to find faith for themselves; they find internal meaning and purpose, and do not need to be with others in church. Theirs is a self-constructed or reconstructed faith, attained on their own, separate from others. They came from churches that did not allow them to question, and they now 'pick and mix' to create their own faith: they hold the conviction 'this is my faith and I own it', and see themselves as people of faith, and as Christians.

'Integrated way-finders' re-connect with like-minded people, and join new types of church group. They find or build their own faith, integrating it with their identity (who they are), lifestyle (how they live), and convictions (what they believe). They have quietly developed a strong, autonomous faith – one that they don't push on to others. They have no agenda to defend, and are secure where they are spiritually. Some are comfortable embracing the values and insights of other faiths – more so than members of any of the other four categories.

Seven people were listed in a small additional category as 'transition to alternative faith': these had joined a 'new age' movement or another faith.

Jamieson claims people left the church not primarily because of its style, or how culturally relevant it was perceived to be, but due to issues of theology and faith. In addition, the leavers perceived that the church lacked a sense of community, and a sense that people knew them personally.

According to Jamieson, the issues arising from his research into church leaving are the church's need to:

- enable members to doubt, question and explore their faith
- devise a theology of 'journey'
- understand the leaving process
- offer assistance to members in their faith struggles
- model a range of theological understandings
- focus on what is real rather than what members 'should' do
- allow more scope for churchgoers' feelings and intuitions

The single most helpful factor for people who had been 're-integrating' their faith was new groups, where theological issues could be discussed, and those exploring their faith could be listened to. The main features of listening which helped those exploring faith were:

- the listening was 'non-judgemental'
- what they said was accepted at 'face-value'
- what they said was accepted as 'provisional'
- they were listened to 'long-term', over an extended period
- the listening was 'incarnational' – the listeners understood the speaker's situation.

Jamieson's follow-up book, *Church Leavers: Faith journeys five years on*, looked at where the leavers where five years later. He quantified the results in percentage terms: the 'disillusioned followers' and 'transitional explorers' – 68%, no change; 'alternative faith transition' – 100%, no change; 'integrated wayfinders' – 90%, no change.[19]

You cannot read the New Testament without realising that some sort of community is vital for sustaining faith. Christians are urged to keep on meeting with other Christians. Hebrews 10:25 is an exhortation to believers who were former Jews tempted back into Judaism: 'Let us not give up meeting together ... let us encourage one another ...' So those who are convinced about the value of congregational life have a point. But, as congregational members, we also have a choice: do we simply shun those who choose not to join a church, or seek to love them in whatever ways we can? An attitude of 'showing them the error of their ways' will merely reinforce the reasons they left in the first place. As far as they are concerned, they are still following Jesus; and some of them see those still 'bound' (as they see it) to traditional congregational life as unable to accomplish what *they* can.

As we have seen, many who have left the Church still attend conferences, worship celebrations and the like, but have little opportunity for fellowship with other believers. Most Christian gatherings are church-based, and it would be hard for a leaver to attend without feeling they are being 'brought back' into the church. Maybe churches, or groups of churches, need to offer gatherings where people can come to explore faith issues with 'no strings attached'; this could be a welcome option for those who have left church life behind, but would still value contact with other Christians.

Questions for discussion

1. What would you like to see happen in your church?
2. Did one of the approaches you have read about in this chapter have particular resonance for you? Did you think, 'If only our church could be like that'?
3. What implications does each of these future church styles have for pastoral care?
4. Are any of the trends discussed here evident in the church you attend?
5. What are your church's strengths and weaknesses?
   What opportunities and threats does your church face?

Where are you now?

In this chapter we have outlined some of the major new approaches to church life in the UK. Some additional questions might help you to think through your response.

1. If things continue as they are, what would you envisage to be the size and *composition* of your church (i) in ten years' time? (ii) in twenty years' time?
2. Do you think God is leading you in a particular direction? For example, by a particular prompting or revelation you have received, ideas suggested to you, conferences or seminars you have attended, or churches you have visited?
3. What influence does the secular world have on your planning and activities as a church?
4. In carrying out its ministry, to what degree is your church inward-focused, and to what degree is it *outward*-focused?
5. How necessary is it for your church to change its approach?
   ☐ Not at all   ☐ Fairly important   ☐ Essential
6. How important is it for your church to change its theological emphasis?
   ☐ Not at all   ☐ Fairly important   ☐ Essential
7. Which area of your church life needs most urgent attention?
   Agreement on the way forward
   A sense of God's presence
   Leadership structures
   Leadership styles
   Conflict resolution
   Personal growth
   Finances
   Buildings
   Theology
   Outreach
8. Reflecting on the three broad options for change, which way is your church likely to go:
   ☐ Stick with the past?   ☐ Evaluate the present?
   ☐ Equip for the future?

9. What are the key reasons for your answer to question 8 above? Consider the following:

    We are not experiencing problems at present

    We are committed to our current theology and practices, so are unlikely to change

    We are definitely in need of change

    We are sure that if we don't do something radical, our church will not make headway in the new climate

    God has shown us very clearly the approach we need to take

    We have a leadership who are committed to the approach we need

    We have a pastor/vicar/senior leader who is committed to the approach we need

    We are not the sort of church that thinks deeply about these things

    We don't have the quality of leadership to do what is needed

    There are constraints on what we can do within our denomination/ church stream

    We are ignorant of how much we have to change, and what is required

10. Which route would be most popular, if the church members understood the three options in question 8 above?

11. Which route would you personally prefer?

12. In the light of your answers so far, what do you need to do? Consider the following:

    Start a series of meetings outlining the need for change in a particular area

    Gather a group of like-minded people to brainstorm the next move

    Make this an agenda item at the next members' meeting

    Visit churches who are doing what we aspire to do

    Invite someone to help us re-envision the church

    Start implementing changes immediately

    Talk with leaders in the church

    Call the church to prayer

    Call a meeting

YOUR NEXT STEP

As the saying goes, 'Tomorrow is the first day of the rest of your life'. It is also true that tomorrow is the first day of the rest of your church's life. For many churches, the realisation that 'we can't go on like this' demands that we think seriously about changing, to be better prepared for the future.

The subject matter of this book deserves a serious response. In life we all have defining moments that can change the course of our lives. For us it may not be the news that our life will be cut short: but it may be that the local church we know and love is going to die. This book has been written as a guide for your thinking in this area. Its benefit will be enhanced as church leaders talk together about their church's situation, identify the relevant factors, and prayerfully consider solutions.

You are about to finish and perhaps, like me, you have closed a book with good intentions of taking action – only to come across that book gathering dust months later, your resolutions forgotten.

Here are some factors that will help you if you are serious about change:

A sense of God's direction

There's nothing more compelling to bring change than the sense that God is leading you. Beyond clever ideas, and the imitation of the great and the good worldwide, we all need to sense that God has His hand on our particular congregation, and that as leaders we are merely co-operating with what He is doing. This 'sense of God's direction' comes in many ways, and we are convinced that God is gracious in helping us to move forward, showing us the way clearly. For some churches there is a troubling awareness that 'unless God does something, we are sunk' – a healthy place to start. For others, a crisis may emerge from a church split, or a minister/vicar/pastor leaving initiates a period of self-examination. In other churches, members may sense that God is speaking through regular preaching, prophetic words, or a leader – bishop, superintendent, or apostolic leader. Some people may even sense God's direction as they read a book like this one.

Of course, hearing God is no guarantee that His voice will be heeded. Many churches have heard what they should do but not done it, and – like the children of Israel – find themselves in the wilderness until they are finally prepared to obey God (and hopefully before those who first heard God's call 'die in the desert'!).

If your church has seen a significant number of members leave, then you can guarantee that the Lord of your church will have something to say about it. Perhaps discerning God's will might be a topic for a church-wide prayer time, or a focus of leadership team discussion?

A determination to fight spiritual entropy

Entropy is the term for the inherent tendency in any natural process for useful energy to dissipate. Christians applying the concept to the church notice that the natural tendency of members is to do nothing and focus on ourselves. Mark Mittelberg, in his book *Building a Contagious Church*,[1] writes of the way in which evangelism is so quickly off the agenda because we all tend to look inward rather than using our energy in the Spirit-driven cause of reaching out to others. We can all find a good reason for doing nothing. You are reading this book, and perhaps there is a good chance that you are disposed to action in your church, especially on the matter of 'back-door loss', but there are always some Christians who will argue that – real though the problem is – now is not the time for action. Here are some common 'entropic' responses to the need for change, along with a question to challenge each one:

- We aren't ready for change. (So when exactly will we be ready?)
- It's not a big issue. (Have you seen the church-leaving statistics?)
- We're doing OK. (But we could be doing better!)
- We might upset some people. (That's true with any change; and it's not a valid reason for not doing what's right.)
- We can't afford to. (Can we afford not to?)
- We aren't sure exactly what to do. (God will lead us as we try different strategies.)
- We tried it before. (That was then – this is now.)
- We haven't tried it before. (So why not try it now?)

This book has emphasised the importance of leaders listening to church members, and where possible taking them with you. But good leadership may include a vision of the future which followers may not see: a leader with a vision should not be deterred by myopic members, when a brighter future awaits the church.

Matching belief and practice

Our behaviour is an outcome of our beliefs. My belief in prayer is demonstrated by the amount of time I spend praying. Similarly, you may have beliefs about your church, and what you actually do will show what you believe. As a leader you can't really believe in salvation through grace by faith, if you preach that moral improvement is the way to get to heaven. You can't really believe in reaching people with the gospel if you do nothing to encourage your members to *communicate* the gospel.

Churches that take back-door loss seriously will examine what they say they believe, and consider whether they really practise it; they will also assess what their present practices (and these may include reasons for loss of members) demonstrate about their true beliefs. Our suspicion is that many Christians would be challenged by such self-examination – we know we are – and that many churches would be shocked if they compared their regular activities with their stated beliefs.

Humility in assessing how things are

Opposing God is never wise but many do so, if only unconsciously. James quotes Proverbs 3:34: 'God opposes the proud but gives grace to the humble' (James 4:6).

I wrote an article for *Christianity* magazine about mega-churches in the UK, having talked to the leader of a London mega-church. His church was very successful, and many minsters envied its membership growth. What impressed me was the pastor's sheer humility at his church's success, and his refusal to stop at that level. 'In our neighbourhood, many people still don't know Christ,' he said. 'There is no room for complacency.'

It may be difficult for leaders to analyse how they are leading a church, and envisage how they could do it better. It is hard when leaders see back-door loss as a tangible sign of their failure. Loss of members has a humbling effect in itself. But even for churches which have grown, the leaders and members can stay humble enough to cry to God for continued guidance and energy. Their attitude can be: 'We may be doing OK, but how could we do better?'

If Christ's gospel touched your church community, what would it look like? How could a revolution of love flood your church membership? How could the lost, the last and the least be welcomed into your church building? What would it take for the Holy Spirit to be truly welcome, to lead your meetings?

Churches that are humble before God discover the truth of James's words: 'Humble yourselves before the Lord, and he will lift you up' (James 4:10).

A concern to advance the gospel

Any football fan will tell you that the best form of defence is attack. I hope this book has conveyed a little of the sense that Jesus is building His Church, and that although some people may be leaving out of the back door, many are coming through the front – and staying. A 'siege mentality' of protecting the little we have is never a good idea – ask any football fan whose team tries to defend a one-nil lead. One of the surest ways to build momentum within a church family is to have a sense of 'missional purpose': a conviction that God has placed you where you are so that you can further His purposes in the world, and join the exciting co-operative venture that He intends for His people. As Frost and Hirsch put it succinctly: 'Don't think church, think mission.'[2]

Perhaps you don't have any children in your church: so how could you bring some in? Sunday isn't a good day for children: well, what could you offer midweek?

You don't know any children: well, make your church known to them – how about offering a homework club, or a holiday club?[3]

Mission will always drive us back to God, and make us ask Him how we should work. Many churches remain static and sterile because they haven't woken up to what God has called them to be and do. The Holy Spirit will always thrust us out into mission, if we are willing. We may be delighted by a sense of His presence in worship, but if we are not sent by Him into mission, we should question how genuine our relationship with Him really is. The Spirit longs to make Jesus known, and will use you if you ask Him to show you how.

A commitment to do whatever it takes, for as long as it takes

It hardly needs saying that change often takes time. But change can come quickly. One church described in this book was unrecognisable after three months. However, broad and long-lasting change usually takes a while, especially if a church culture has been embedded for years. I want to emphasise this point because I know how long God has had to wait for me to adjust to what He wanted me to do. Change is not for the faint-hearted or casual. It may take years for a congregation to become not inward-looking passengers, but a vibrant outward-looking mission centre. What will keep us going is the sense that God is leading us on, and that we have chosen to be His disciples, following His voice and caring for His Church of which we are part.

In May 2009, Sir Ranulph Fiennes finally climbed Mount Everest, making him the first explorer in history who had reached the world's highest peak as well as the North and South Poles, and also the oldest Briton and the first British pensioner to do so. He did it on his third attempt, having been unsuccessful in 2005 and 2008.

Fiennes famously suffers from vertigo and says he looks up, but never down. He kept going up the mountain by repeating two mantras he had prepared: 'plod forever', and 'die high'.

Perhaps Sir Ranulph provides a picture of the sort of churches that will prevail in the days to come: churches that will do whatever it takes, for as long as it takes – 'plod forever', if necessary. The great news is that we do not have to depend on our human resilience, but on a Lord and master who says, as he told Peter:

> 'And I tell you that you are Peter, and on this rock I will build my church, and the gates of Hades will not overcome it.' (Matt. 16:18)

FURTHER READING

MUST-READ BOOKS

Tom Sine, *The New Conspirators: Creating the Future One Mustard Seed at a Time* (Downers Grove, IL: IVP, 2008)
(A thoughtful, wide-ranging and analytical review from an author with decades of experience and reflection in this field.)

David Kinnaman and Gabe Lyons, *UnChristian: What a New Generation Really Thinks About the Church ... and Why it Matters* (Grand Rapids, MI: Baker, 2007)
(Though this book is based on US research, many of its findings apply to the Church in the UK. You cannot read this book and remain detached or unchallenged.)

Alan Jamieson, *A Churchless Faith: Faith Journeys Beyond the Churches* (London: SPCK, 2002)
(Based on PhD research; valuable for understanding the journeys of those who leave church.)

Alan Jamieson, Jenny McIntosh and Adrienne Thompson, *Church Leavers: Faith journeys five years on* (London: SPCK, 2006)

Alan Jamieson, *Chrysalis: Faith in an Emerging Culture* (Carlisle: Paternoster Press, 2008)

Jason Gardner, *Mend the Gap: Can the Church Reconnect the Generations?* (Nottingham: IVP, 2008)
(Jason has researched this topic thoroughly, and the book makes compelling and insightful reading.)

George Barna, *Revolution* (Carol Stream: Tyndale, 2005)

Eddie Gibbs and Ryan K. Bolger, *Emerging Churches: Creating Christian Community in Postmodern Cultures* (Grand Rapids, MI: Baker, 2005)

Eddie Gibbs and Ian Coffey, *Church Next: Quantum Changes in Christian Ministry* (Leicester: IVP, 2000)

Scot McKnight, *The Jesus Creed* (Brewster, MA: Paraclete, 2004)

OTHER BOOKS RELEVANT TO THE 21ST- CENTURY CHURCH
Harry Blamires, *The Post-Christian Mind* (Ann Arbor, MI: Servant, 1999)

D.A. Carson, *Becoming Conversant with the Emerging Church* (Grand Rapids, MI: Zondervan, 2005)

Tim Chester and Steve Timmis, *Total Church: A Radical Reshaping around Gospel and Community* (Nottingham: IVP, 2007)

Michael Frost and Alan Hirsch, *The Shaping of Things to Come: Innovation and Mission for the Twenty-first-century Church* (Peabody, MA: Hendrickson, 2003)

Mark Greene and Tracy Cotterell (eds), *Let my People Grow* (London: LICC, 2006)

A.J. Kiesling, *Jaded: Hope for Believers who have Given up on Church but not on God* (Grand Rapids, MI: Baker, 2004)

Brian D. McLaren, *The Church on the Other Side – Doing Ministry in the Postmodern Matrix* (Grand Rapids: Zondervan, 1998)

Stuart Murray, *Post-Christendom: Church and Mission in a Strange World* (Milton Keynes: Paternoster, 2004)

David Murrow, *Why Men Hate Going to Church* (Nashville: Thomas Nelson, 2005)

Michael Nazir-Ali, *Shapes of the Church to Come* (Eastbourne: Kingsway, 2001)

Tim Sudworth, Graham Cray and Chris Russell, *Mission-shaped Youth: Rethinking Young People and the Church* (London: Church House, 2007)

Viv Thomas, *Future Leader* (Carlisle: Paternoster, 1999)

NOTES

FOREWORD

1. Graham Tomlin, *The Provocative Church* (London: SPCK, 2002) p.10.
2. Tom Wright, *Surprised by Hope* (London: SPCK, 2007) p.119

INTRODUCTION

1. Peter Brierley, *Pulling Out of the Nosedive* (London: Christian Research, 2006), pp.12–14.
2. Monica Furlong, *The C. of E.: The State It's In* (London: Hodder and Stoughton, 2000), pp.216–217.
3. According to Christian Research, 'New Churches' saw a 10% decline from 1998 to 2005. Between 2001 and 2006 black church membership grew by about 18%, compared with a 5% drop for churches nationally. http://news.bbc.co.uk/1/hi/uk/4704925.stm, accessed 1 June 2009.
4. Robin Gill, *The Empty Church Revisited* (Aldershot: Ashgate Publishing, 2003), p.162.
5. Alison Park, *British Social Attitudes 2006/2007* (London: SAGE Publications, 2008), p.9.
6. Tearfund research, 'Churchgoing in the UK', 3 April 2007. The survey involved 7,000 UK adults aged 16 or over, interviewed between 8 February and 5 March 2006.
7. From a conversation with George Lings, director of the Sheffield Centre, the research arm of the Church Army. He actually said that 40% was an optimistic figure.
8. Mori poll results, 8–17 August 2003. Poll data: www.ipsos-mori.com/polls/2003/bbc-heavenandearth-top.shtml and summary: www.ipsos-mori.com/polls/2003/bbc-heavenandearth.shtml.
9. Martyn Percy, *Engaging with Contemporary Culture: Christianity, Theology and the Concrete Church* (Aldershot: Ashgate Publishing, 2005), p.62.

CHAPTER 1

1. Wolfgang Simson, *Houses That Change the World: The Return of the House Churches* (Milton Keynes: Authentic Lifestyle, 2001), p.81.
2. Office for National Statistics 2001 April Census Summary of Religion in Britain, released 2003.
3. *Manchester Evening News* (9 June 2008).
4. World Values Survey quoted at http://www.usatoday.com/news/world/2005-08-10-europe-religion-cover_x.htm, accessed 1 June 2009.
5. George Barna, *Revolution* (Ventura, CA: Barna Books, 2005).

CHAPTER 2

1. Church growth researchers say that if we have five good friends we are likely to stay in a church even if there's something we really don't like about it. We haven't been able to verify this, but have heard it quoted many times.

2. Nick Spencer, *Where Do We Go From Here? A Biblical Perspective on Mobility* (Cambridge: the Jubilee Centre, 2003). Available online at: http://www.jubilee-centre.org.

3. See The *Daily Telegraph*, 3 September 2008, www.telegraph.co.uk, accessed 1 June 2009.

4. Quoted to me by Martin Saunders, editor of *Youthwork*, on 'The Leadership File', Premier Christian Radio, in 2007.

5. Jason Gardner, *Mend The Gap* (Nottingham: IVP, 2008), p.73.

6. Philip Richter and Leslie Francis, *Gone but not Forgotten* (London: Darton, Longman and Todd, 1998). The comment by Professor Francis was in a *Church Times* article, 'Inviting people back to the future church', 28 September 2007, http://www.churchtimes.co.uk/content.asp?id=45190.

7. Philip Richter and Leslie Francis, op. cit. and Philip Richter and Leslie Francis, *Gone for Good? Church Leaving and Returning in the Twenty-first Century* (Doncaster: Epworth, 2007).

8. Michael Frost and Alan Hirsch, *The Shaping of Things to Come: Innovation and Mission for the Twenty-first-century Church* (Edinburgh: Hendrickson Publishers, 2003).

9. If you have been affected by this, you may find Marc Dupont's book helpful: *Toxic Churches: Restoration from Spiritual Abuse* (Grand Rapids, MI: Chosen, 2004).

10. *Pulling Out of the Nosedive* (London: Christian Research, 2006). The spurious reasons include: parking facilities, other churches in catchment area, church location, distance to travel, bus routes, attractiveness of church building, academic acumen of church, income of church, Alpha courses, size of congregation, cell groups, presence of young people, students at local college, and associated schools.

11. Ibid., p.206.

12. Frank R. Tillapaugh, *The Church Unleashed* (Ventura, CA: Regal, 1982), p.81.

CHAPTER 3

1. See Rob Hay, Valerie Lim, Detlef Blocher, Jaap Ketelaar and Sarah Hay (eds), *Worth Keeping: Global Perspectives on Best Practice in Missionary Retention* (Pasadena, CA: World Evangelical Alliance and William Carey Library, 2007). The research includes the finding that 80% of people who go into mission not expecting to lead end up in some kind of leadership position. Annual attrition could be halved if the missions learned best practice from high-retaining agencies, including helping mission leaders to lead more effectively.

2. See CWR's website www.cwr.org.uk for a gift assessment chart. Also Bruce Bugbee, Don Cousins and Bill Hybels, *Network Revised Curriculum*, DVD (Grand Rapids, MI: Zondervan, 2004); Erik Rees, *Shape: Finding and Fulfilling your Unique Purpose in Life* (Grand Rapids, MI: Zondervan, 2006).

3. Marcus Buckingham and Donald O. Clifton, *Now, Discover Your Strengths* (New York: Simon and Schuster, 2001).

4. See Peter Brierley, *Pulling Out of the Nosedive* (London: Christian Research, 2006), p.166.

5. Martin Saunders, *Christianity* (February 2009).
6. Tommy Tenney, *The God Chasers* (Shippensburg, PA: Destiny Image Publishers, 1999), pp.2–3.
7. Selwyn Hughes, *7 Laws of Spiritual Success* (Farnham: CWR, 2005).
8. Craig Groeschel, *It: How Churches and Leaders can Get It and Keep It* (Grand Rapids, MI: Zondervan, 2008).
9. Ibid., pp.115, 116.
10. I have heard Bill Hybels use the story twice, once live at a leadership conference in the UK and also on 'Defining Moments', the Willow Creek monthly audio journal for church leaders.
11. George Lakoff and Mark Johnson, *Metaphors We Live By* (Chicago: University of Chicago Press, 1980).
12. At least not in the conventional sense that we use them in the twenty-first century. We are not saying programmes are wrong, merely that the focus of the apostolic teaching is helping people to see who they are in Christ. The programmes seem to assume that appropriate ministry would flow from that basis.
13. James Thwaites, *Church that Works* (Milton Keynes: Authentic Lifestyle, 2003).
14. Jonathan Edwards, *The Works of Jonathan Edwards*, Volume 1 (Edinburgh: Banner of Truth, 1974), p.248.
15. Rick Warren, *Purpose Driven Church* (Grand Rapids, MI: Zondervan, 1995), p.153.
16. See http://www.connexions-direct.com, accessed 1 June 2009.
17. Philip Greenslade, *A Passion for God's Story* (Carlisle: Paternoster, 2006).
18. N.T. Wright, *The Last Word: Scripture and the Authority of God – Getting Beyond the Bible Wars* (London: HarperOne, 2006), p.124.
19. Ibid., pp.124–5.
20. Stephen R. Covey, *Seven Habits of Highly Effective People* (New York: Free Press, 1990), pp.81–5.

CHAPTER 4

1. We look at research by Alan Jamieson presented in *A Churchless Faith: Faith Journeys Beyond the Churches* (London: SPCK, 2002) in Chapter 5.
2. Quoted by Scot McKnight, 'Five Streams of the Emerging Church' (*Christianity Today*, February 2007, Vol. 51, No. 2, and available online at http://www.christianitytoday.com/ct/2007/february/11.35.html?start=6, accessed 1 June 2009.
3. D.A. Carson *The Gagging of God: Christianity Confronts Pluralism* (Grand Rapids, MI: Zondervan, 2002). The book provides a good critique of postmodernism and pluralism. It is a useful place to start if you want to explore these issues.
4. David Kinnaman and Gabe Lyons, *UnChristian: What a New Generation Really Thinks about Christianity ... and Why it Matters* (Grand Rapids, MI: Baker Books, 2007).

CHAPTER 5

1. We look at 'emerging Church' later in the chapter. It is a loose and broad term reflecting a postmodern approach to life with Christ.
2. Andy Freeman and Pete Greig, *Punk Monk: New Monasticism and the Ancient Art of Breathing* (Milton Keynes: Authentic Media, 2008).
3. Rick Warren, *The Purpose Driven Life: What on Earth am I Here For?* (Grand Rapids, MI: Zondervan, 2002).
4. www.kt.org.
5. For a history of this, you might try an excellent description by Andrew Walker, *Restoring the Kingdom* (London: Eagle Publishing, 1998).
6. Randy Clark said this in a question-and-answer session at the Central Hall, Southampton, where he led a healing and impartation conference from 22 to 25 April 2009.
7. Eddie Gibbs and Ryan K. Bolger, *Emerging Churches: Creating Community in Postmodern Cultures* (Grand Rapids, MI: Baker Academic, 2005).
8. Ibid., p.236.
9. Tom Sine, *The New Conspirators: Creating the Future One Mustard Seed at a Time* (Downers Grove, IL: IVP, 2008).
10. www.freshexpressions.org.uk, accessed 1 June 2009.
11. Michael Frost and Alan Hirsch, *The Shaping of Things to Come: Innovation and Mission for the Twenty-first-century Church* (Edinburgh: Hendrickson Publishers, 2003), p.18.
12. Ibid., pp.114–15.
13. Ibid., p.83.
14. Rene Padilla, *Mission Between the Times* (Grand Rapids: Eerdmans, 1985) p.93.
15. Peter Brierley, *Pulling Out of the Nosedive* (London: Christian Research, 2006), p.153.
16. http://www.bible.ca/global-religion-statistics-world-christian-encyclopedia.htm.
17. George Barna, www.barna.org, accessed 1 June 2009.
18. Alan Jamieson, *A Churchless Faith: Faith Journeys Beyond the Churches* (London: SPCK, 2002). See also a helpful summary of a talk Alan gave on this topic in 2004 at http://www.emergentuk.org, which I found helpful as I researched this part of the chapter.
19. Ibid., p.81.

CHAPTER 6

1. Mark Mittelberg, *Building a Contagious Church* (Grand Rapids, MI: Zondervan, 2000), p.106.
2. Michael Frost and Alan Hirsch, *The Shaping of Things to Come: Innovation and Mission for the Twenty-first-century Church* (Edinburgh: Hendrickson Publishers, 2003), p.81.
3. But beware that holiday clubs often merely entertain children, but don't add to the church. When working at *Christianity* magazine we spoke with a number of leaders who had put a lot of time and effort into such ventures but seen little lasting fruit, valuable though the club was at the time.

NATIONAL DISTRIBUTORS

UK: (and countries not listed below)
CWR, Waverley Abbey House, Waverley Lane, Farnham, Surrey GU9 8EP.
Tel: (01252) 784700 Outside UK (44) 1252 784700

AUSTRALIA: CMC Australasia, PO Box 519, Belmont, Victoria 3216.
Tel: (03) 5241 3288 Fax: (03) 5241 3290

CANADA: David C Cook Distribution Canada, PO Box 98, 55 Woodslee Avenue,
Paris, Ontario N3L 3E5. Tel: 1800 263 2664

GHANA: Challenge Enterprises of Ghana, PO Box 5723, Accra.
Tel: (021) 222437/223249 Fax: (021) 226227

HONG KONG: Cross Communications Ltd, 1/F, 562A Nathan Road, Kowloon.
Tel: 2780 1188 Fax: 2770 6229

INDIA: Crystal Communications, 10-3-18/4/1, East Marredpalli, Secunderabad –
500026, Andhra Pradesh. Tel/Fax: (040) 27737145

KENYA: Keswick Books and Gifts Ltd, PO Box 10242-00400, Nairobi.
Tel: (254) 20 312639/3870125

MALAYSIA: Salvation Book Centre (M) Sdn Bhd, 23 Jalan SS 2/64, 47300 Petaling
Jaya, Selangor. Tel: (03) 78766411/78766797 Fax: (03) 78757066/78756360

Canaanland, No. 25 Jalan PJU 1A/41B, NZX Commercial Centre, Ara Jaya,
47301 Petaling Jaya, Selangor. Tel: (03) 7885 0540/1/2 Fax: (03) 7885 0545

NEW ZEALAND: CMC Australasia, PO Box 303298, North Harbour,
Auckland 0751. Tel: 0800 449 408 Fax: 0800 449 049

NIGERIA: FBFM, Helen Baugh House, 96 St Finbarr's College Road, Akoka, Lagos.
Tel: (01) 7747429/4700218/825775/827264

PHILIPPINES: OMF Literature Inc, 776 Boni Avenue, Mandaluyong City.
Tel: (02) 531 2183 Fax: (02) 531 1960

SINGAPORE: Alby Commercial Enterprises Pte Ltd, 95 Kallang Avenue #04-00,
AIS Industrial Building, 339420. Tel: (65) 629 27238 Fax: (65) 629 27235

SOUTH AFRICA: Struik Christian Books, 80 MacKenzie Street, PO Box 1144,
Cape Town 8000. Tel: (021) 462 4360 Fax: (021) 461 3612

SRI LANKA: Christombu Publications (Pvt) Ltd, Bartleet House,
65 Braybrooke Place, Colombo 2. Tel: (9411) 2421073/2447665

USA: David C Cook Distribution Canada, PO Box 98, 55 Woodslee Avenue, Paris,
Ontario N3L 3E5, Canada. Tel: 1800 263 2664

For email addresses, visit the CWR website: www.cwr.org.uk

Day and Residential Courses
Counselling Training
Leadership Development
Biblical Study Courses
Regional Seminars
Ministry to Women
Daily Devotionals
Books and Videos
Conference Centre

Trusted all Over the World

CWR HAS GAINED A WORLDWIDE reputation as a centre of excellence for Bible-based training and resources. From our headquarters at Waverley Abbey House, Farnham, England, we have been serving God's people for over 40 years with a vision to help apply God's Word to everyday life and relationships. The daily devotional *Every Day with Jesus* is read by nearly a million readers an issue in more than 150 countries, and our unique courses in biblical studies and pastoral care are respected all over the world. Waverley Abbey House provides a conference centre in a tranquil setting.

For free brochures on our seminars and courses, conference facilities, or a catalogue of CWR resources, please contact us at the following address.
CWR, Waverley Abbey House, Waverley Lane, Farnham, Surrey GU9 8EP, UK

Telephone: +44 (0)1252 784719
Email: mail@cwr.org.uk
Website: www.cwr.org.uk

CWR Applying God's Word
to everyday life and relationships

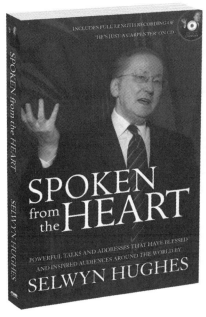
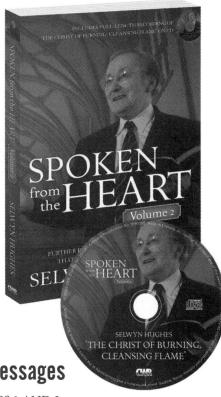

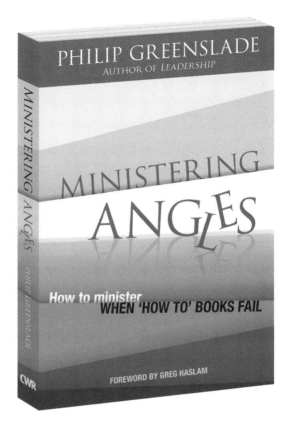

Be empowered for fruitful service

MINISTERING ANGLES

Whether you teach, oversee, counsel, advise, evangelise, care for or pray
for others in the Church, this compendium of insights will give you much
food for thought. Discover from Jeremiah, Jesus, Paul and others how the
counter cultural call to be a 'wounded healer', a 'wise fool' and a 'competent
inadequate' can empower you for more effective and fruitful service.

by Philip Greenslade
Format: 266-page paperback, 153 x 230mm
ISBN: 978-1-85345-522-3
£15.99

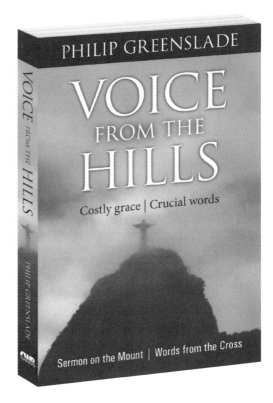

Find the power to be more holy

VOICE FROM THE HILLS – COSTLY GRACE, CRUCIAL WORDS

Discover some surprising links between the Sermon on the Mount and Christ's seven 'words' from the cross. You will be challenged and empowered by the Holy Spirit afresh as you understand why 'it takes nothing less than the cross of God's Son to implement in us the Sermon on the Mount'.

by Philip Greenslade
Format: 234-page paperback, 172 x 230mm
ISBN: 978-1-85345-469-1
£9.99

Life is not a rehearsal

A LIFE TO DIE FOR

From the very first line, author Andy Peck challenges us to recognise
the part we can play in God's strategic plan for the renewal of creation.
Powerfully illustrated by contemporary books and films, this is a
biblically grounded and highly practical call to radical discipleship.

by Andy Peck
Format: 168-page paperback, 153 x 231mm
ISBN: 978-1-85345-443-1
£8.99

Buy online at **www.cwrstore.org.uk** or call +44 (0)1252 784710.
Also available from your local Christian bookshop.
Price correct at time of printing and exclusive of p&p.